You Are Stronger Than You Think:
Lessons of Endurance in the Race of Faith

Kendra Tillman

Unless otherwise indicated, all Scripture quotations are taken from the Holy Bible, New Living Translation, copyright © 1996, 2004, 2007 by Tyndale House Foundation. Used by permission of Tyndale House Publishers, Inc., Carol Stream, Illinois 60188. All rights reserved.

Scripture quotations marked (AMP) are taken from the Amplified® Bible, Copyright © 1954, 1958, 1962, 1964, 1965, 1987 by The Lockman Foundation. Used by permission. (www.Lockman.org)

Scripture quotations marked (MSG) are taken from The Message. Copyright © 1993, 1994, 1995, 1996, 2000, 2001, 2002. Used by permission of NavPress Publishing Group.

Scripture quotations marked (NASB) are taken from the NEW AMERICAN STANDARD BIBLE®, Copyright © 1960,1962,1963,1968,1971,1972,1973,1975,1977,1995 by The Lockman Foundation. Used by permission.

THE HOLY BIBLE, NEW INTERNATIONAL VERSION®, NIV® Copyright © 1973, 1978, 1984, 2011 by Biblica, Inc.® Used by permission. All rights reserved worldwide.

Copyright © 2015 Kendra Tillman

All rights reserved.

ISBN-13: 978-0996356701
ISBN-10: 0996356703

DEDICATION

I dedicate this book to my parents, my husband and our three children.

To my parents, you have been living, breathing examples to me for 39 years of what it means to be stronger than I think. Mama, as a young girl, I'm sure teen mother is not what you imagined for your future. Yet, when that became your reality, you had enough fight in you to keep reaching for a way out of a life of poverty. Daddy, thank you for stepping up to be my Dad and helping me see that stepchild doesn't mean less than. I am forever grateful to you both for your love and your example.

To our children, Nyah, Nathan and Jonathan, you will be the legacy your Dad and I leave this world. The words of this book are my attempt to collect the wisdom I've learned in my 39 years of living on this earth. I pray you will learn from my mistakes, as much as from my successes. May God use these words as a source of encouragement for you (and everyone who reads it).

To my husband, Daniel, I am so thankful for the man that you are and the husband you have been to me for 18 years. Thank you for loving me unconditionally and being my loudest, most consistent supporter through the years. You are my hero.

PRAISE FOR
YOU ARE STRONGER THAN YOU THINK

"Kendra has just given you a road map to successfully accomplish any goal you have. Sometimes it is challenging to start a project and even more difficult to finish it. Read this book if you are stuck, frustrated, or stopped trying. Go back to this book when you need motivation and encouragement that you aren't alone in this journey and that you too can experience victory."
Ericka Young, tailormadebudgets.com
Financial Coach and Budgeting Expert

"This is a dynamic book full of inspiration for the person who understands that they are full of destiny and purpose, but has obstacles to overcome. *You are Stronger Than You Think* is just what you need shoot adrenalin into your soul so that you can continue to "do life" full of confident expectation that your best days are ahead of you. This book is full of practical, yet, profound principles that will assist you in bouncing back after a setback. It includes stories of triumph and encouragement that will help you to realize that no matter what may come your way, you can handle it because you are stronger than you think."
Minister Erica Moore, fcc-phx.com
Co-Pastor of Faith Christian Center, Phoenix and
the Founder of Woman2Woman Online Book Club

"As we continue to run the race of faith, life, and marriage we are reminded in this book that procrastination, comparison, complacency and shame can knock us off our feet. But you'll forever be equipped with great training tools Kendra gives you! If you feel like you are in the wrong assignment in life this is a must read today!"
Dena Patton, denapatton.com
Business coach. Speaker. Best-selling author.

CONTENTS

	Introduction	1

SECTION I: The Starting Line

1	Lesson: It All Begins with God	7
2	Lesson: Everything Would Be Different If You Changed	21

SECTION II: The Race of Faith

3	Lesson: The Runner's Secret…Endurance	45
4	Lesson: Be Ready to Run	56
5	Lesson: Persevere in Your Most Valued Relationships	75
6	Lesson: Having It All Is Exhausting!	94
7	Lesson: Run Your Own Race!	103
8	Lesson: Finish Strong!	114

INTRODUCTION

I love this Erma Bombeck quote: "When I stand before God at the end of my life, I would hope that I would not have a single bit of talent left, and could say, 'I used everything you gave me.'"

That's how I want to live. I want to live a life of no regrets.

Regret steals hope. It slowly erodes our confidence. Over time it quietly bullies us to give up before we reach our potential. If you've ever felt tempted or succumbed to the temptation to give up in an area of your life, you've been bullied by regret.

Regret wastes time. *We spend years regretting moments* we can never get back instead of focusing on the life we have before us.

Regret blinds us to lessons that could keep us from repeating mistakes. It keeps us from gleaning what we can from our circumstances. Just this week my tween daughter encountered a mean girl. As we talked about what happened, I asked her, "What did you learn?" Her response was that everyone is not going to like her. "True," I replied, "but what did you learn about yourself? How will you respond differently the next time you encounter a mean girl?" My questions offended her because she felt I was blaming her. She couldn't tell me what she learned about herself or how to respond the next time. I asked her those questions not because I felt she had done anything wrong. I asked because I know once she learns to extract life's lessons from situations, she won't walk away from them with worry or regret. How many of us as adults live in a state of regret simply because we haven't learned to draw out the lesson?

God does not want *you* to live a life of regret.

To not live in regret or fear that my past determines the beauty or success of my future, has been one of my life's greatest lessons. I've failed at so many things so many times, and it's been hard to get back up again and be willing to fight another day. When I allow my mind to focus on where I could be in certain areas of my life, if I had just kept going, I'm overwhelmed by feelings of regret. If I allow myself to wallow in those negative thoughts, I miss out on all the good that is happening now.

So I've decided instead:

I'll never give up.

I'll never give up believing.

I'll never give up believing that I can reach my goal weight.

I'll never give up believing that I can lead and build a successful business.

I'll never give up believing that my children will follow God all the days of their lives.

I'll never give up believing that my husband and I will always have a strong, healthy marriage.

I'll never give up believing writing this book is in God's plan for my life.

I'll never give up believing God intends to keep using me to help women reach full maturity in their potential.

Living a safe life is not now and has never been the goal. Life is messy. It does not fit into the pages of a book, planner or calendar. How do I know?

How can there be hundreds—maybe even thousands—of books on setting and achieving goals? There's really no recipe for success. You can follow all the steps in all the books, and the results will not look the same for you as for someone else. But the one requirement for all forms of success is a willingness to keep moving forward, even when it looks and feels like you can't take another step.

You Are Stronger Than You Think is a book about finishing—and finishing strong—in this race of life. It's about reaching for the finish line without regret and worry weighing you down.

I believe the cure for a life of regret is building our endurance, our faith muscles. Endurance is the unseen force we need to complete anything we start. We need endurance to follow God's leading, to stay married, to raise our children, to nurture our relationships, to complete daily tasks, and to accomplish future goals. God completes what He starts and He wants us to finish what we start.

As I was writing this book, I was amazed to discover how many scriptures speak about remaining strong in this race of faith. God reminds us continually in scripture that He is the source of our strength and we are not on this journey alone. One of my goals in writing this book was for the wisdom God has provided in the scriptures to be at the center of any solutions I offered. In the last 21 years, as a woman of faith, I've found that wisdom for every problem we will encounter can be found in the pages of the Bible. Our specific situations may not be spelled out, but the principles for how to respond to life's tests are there.

My prayer for you as you read this book is that God will remind you of the power, the ability, the greatness on the inside of you, and that you will experience renewed strength and enthusiasm for the life you've been given.

Water Station

I don't want you to forge ahead through these chapters. This race of faith is a test of endurance—which means it's a long-distance race, not a sprint. In a long-distance race you stop at water stations along the way to rehydrate. Within each chapter I've placed a **Water Station** exercise to help you slow down and reflect on what you've read so far. As you slow down to take stock of what you've read, ask yourself, "How can I use it to rehydrate, as I continue to run the race of faith?"

Writing this book has been one of the hardest things I've ever done and my personal test of endurance. In writing these pages, I've had to live out what I've written. The writing and the living it out have made me better, stronger and more sure of what I've written. This isn't a book of theory or lofty ideals. It's me sharing what I've sweated out, heart and soul, over many years. What I share with you may not be groundbreaking, but it can be life-changing if you decide to apply it. I pray that as you read this book, you will not just change behaviors but will allow God to change your heart. *Let's move forward together and fulfill our greatest potential.*

THE STARTING LINE

CHAPTER 1

Lesson: It All Begins with God

My appreciation for running began in elementary school. Do you remember field days? I always loved competing against the other kids in the races. In high school I took up mid-distance running. I wasn't fast enough to be a sprinter and I didn't have the stamina for long distance running. I ended running the race no one else on our team wanted to run-the 800m dash.

Fast forward about thirteen years. I started long distance running, when our two older kids were toddlers. I ran my first 5K in 2004. I remember my first race, because it was the "Year of the Monkey" Run at the Phoenix Zoo. I had trained with a friend for the weeks leading up to it. It was a tough course, but it's probably the fastest 5K I've ever run. I don't remember my exact time, but it was under 30 minutes.

I've also participated in my fair share of boot camps, hikes and group fitness classes at the gym. Despite all of this, I have a secret that may shock my friends. I *don't* love to exercise. Many times, whether I'm in an aerobics class, doing a workout video, or running, I sometimes daydream about stopping, going home, and never coming back. I wish I could say I get lost in the thrill of feeling my body getting stronger. Honestly, I'm usually checking the clock (frequently) to see if my workout is almost over.

I first heard the phrase "You're stronger than you think" during a heart-pounding, difficult strength-training class. Our instructor had no sympathy for our excuses. She wanted you to hold the plank position longer than you thought you could or curl that bicep more times than you felt possible. She motivated you to dig deeper. She could sense our fatigue. She knew it was hard, but she would still reassure us: "You're stronger than you think."

That simple phrase has held so much meaning in my life. One of the things I learned in that class was the direct connection between our minds, our bodies and our spirits. Have you noticed what happens when you work out or do anything physically challenging? Your mind is also challenged. We build our mental toughness (mental endurance, mental stamina or self-discipline) every time we do something that makes us uncomfortable. Our ability to endure also improves any time we are required to deny ourselves of momentary fulfillment for long-term gain. This translates to other areas of our lives. Getting out of bed early to pray and prepare my heart for the day ahead is a form of mental toughness. Reading a story to my toddler at night, when I am exhausted from the day, is a form of mental toughness. Saying "no" to eating out with colleagues five days a week, because it's not good for my budget or my waistline, is also a form of mental toughness. Endurance also develops when we seek to understand our child's perspective, though it would be easier to just have them do what we say. Mental toughness also develops when we choose to forgive someone, knowing our kids are watching and learning from our example. We'll talk more in details about mental stamina in Chapter 4: Be Ready to Run.

It's A Wonderful Life

Strange, isn't it? Each man's life touches so many other lives. And when he isn't around, he leaves an awful hole, doesn't he?

– Clarence, Angel from It's A Wonderful Life

What's one of your favorite movies? You know, the kind that never gets old. You can watch it over and over again like it's the first time. *It's a Wonderful Life* is one of my favorites. Good old, dependable George Bailey is the main character. In the movie George faces a series of setbacks that cause him to want to give up on living. In his desperation he cries out that he wishes he'd never been born. The rest of the movie is about him getting a glimpse of what life would be like for those he knows and loves, if that were true. By the end of the movie he realizes this simple truth: **Our time on this earth is finite, but impactful. We each influence many lives throughout our lifetime without fully understanding the magnitude of our influence.**

George reminds me of another man in history who wondered out loud if never being born was better than dealing with the harsh realities life sometimes brings.

> There is a time for everything,
>
>> and a season for every activity under the heavens:
>>
>> a time to be born and a time to die,
>>
>> a time to plant and a time to uproot,
>>
>> a time to kill and a time to heal,
>>
>> a time to tear down and a time to build,
>>
>> a time to weep and a time to laugh,
>>
>> a time to mourn and a time to dance . . .
>
> He has made everything beautiful in its time. He has also set eternity in the human heart; yet no one can fathom what God has done from beginning to end. I know that there is nothing better for people than to be happy and to do good while they live. That each of them may eat and drink, and find satisfaction in all their toil—this is the gift of God. (Ecclesiastes 3:1-4,11-13)

In chapter 3 of Ecclesiastes, King Solomon, the wisest man who ever lived (according to scripture) reminds himself (and us) of the value of time and the sovereignty of God. As he repeats *time* over and over again, you have to be blind not to catch its significance. Time is precious. It's fleeting. You can't wrap your arms around it. It leaves as quickly as it comes. You don't get any more of it. So, how are you spending it?

Thankfully, we get a fresh serving of grace and mercy every morning. We get to decide how we live the 24 hours we're given each day. Life gets better when we've made up in our minds that it does. It's a wonderful life when you realize God has chosen you. You're not a mistake. Your life is not an accident. It's orchestrated by a purposeful, intentional, life-giving heavenly Father who loves you more than you can imagine.

You may have wondered aloud or inside yourself, *Whom is my life influencing? Am I making a difference?* I may not know you personally, but I can tell you, you're influencing your spouse, your children, your family members, your friends, your neighbors, your children's friends, your colleagues, your employees, your clients, and your customers. The question we have to ask ourselves is, "**H**o*w* are we influencing them?" What legacy are we leaving in our short time on this earth? Stop reading. Grab a pen and paper. Take an inventory of the positive impact you've already made. These successes will continue to inspire you as you press forward with purpose.

Every one of us has a deep need for significance. We all want to know our life matters. It feels natural for our identity to be wrapped up in **what** we do. I think we all hunger to leave a lasting legacy because we were created to do just that. God created that desire, a knowing in us. The problem is when we don't start by going directly to the source for the answers to the longings of our hearts.

For everything, absolutely everything, above and below, visible and invisible ... everything got started in him and finds its purpose in him. (Colossians. 1:16, MSG*)*

Everything and everyone was started in God. We find our purpose in him. Knowing He has a purpose, an intention for why you're here empowers you with a greater strength than what you can create on your own. When you know He has a purpose for your life, you also know that when challenges and setbacks (or even just the mundane things in life) come, you are able to push forward to fulfilling your purpose. Our focus then shifts from **what** we do to **who** we are and **why** we are here.

Observation and experience have taught me, any time we struggle with any type of sin—from laziness to not respecting our bodies—it's because we've lost sight of the greater plan for our lives. You would not be willing to risk wasting your life in a prison cell or living in complacency if you really believed God intends to use your life.

My husband and I are raising a daughter and two sons, and I believe the greatest thing I can teach them is to look to God for their identity. Everything we see and experience that comes from external sources can change. God is our greatest source of stability. He's reliable and dependable. He created each of us with a specific purpose in mind, a purpose that hasn't changed since the day we were born into this world.

One of the benefits of walking with the Lord is learning what He thinks about us. After all, He is the one who created us. Who would know better than He why we are here on this earth? To live fully alive, fully fulfilled and purposeful requires we stay connected to Him. God is our true source of power and identity.

Know Your Strengths

"The greatest tragedy in life is not death, but a life without a purpose. The greatest failure in life is to be successful in the wrong assignment. The greatest mistake in life is to be busy but not effective."[1] *–Dr. Myles Munroe*

In 2014 I pushed fear to the side and decided to pursue a dream that had been in my heart for three years. For three years I'd wanted to host an event for professional women with a Biblical worldview. Why did it take me three years? Fear. I allowed my fear of failure to stop me for three years. In 2014, the year I turned 39, I finally got fed up with fear. After watching Sheryl Sandberg, the COO of Facebook, speak at a women's simulcast[2] about "leaning in," I felt

---

[1] Dr. Myles Munroe, *Applying the Kingdom: Rediscovering the Priority of God for Mankind.* (Destiny Image, 2007)
[2] Take the Lead Launch Event, 2/9/14, http://www.taketheleadwomen.com/take-lead-challenge-launch-event/.

something stir inside of me. I thought what she had to say was interesting, and I wondered what this message meant for professional women who had set the Bible as the foundation for their decision-making. What did the "lean in" message look like for us? Who was helping those of us employed outside of the home part-time or full-time Or those who ran a business from home—those women within the Christian culture who wanted a career and a family and whose primary authority and inspiration was scripture? Who was helping us "lean in"? Should we be "leaning in" in the way Sheryl described it?

I felt fed up with my own complacency. I was fed up with my desire to do something "great for God," but my unwillingness to take a risk at anything I could potentially fail at publicly. I knew I was feeling this way because God wanted me to put some action behind my faith. It was time. It was time for me to abandon the fear of others' opinions to fulfill a calling I knew was from the Lord. I am happy to say God blessed our meeting: September 27th, my 39th birthday and the day of the inaugural "You Are Stronger Than You Think" women's event, was one of the best days of my life. It was amazing to experience all that God did when I shunned doubt and followed Him.

One of the greatest things to come out of the day was our keynote session. I prayed and had a small team of women praying about every aspect of the event. We prayed for every speaker, every attendee, the agenda, the marketing, everything! This small team of women, local and far away, prayed during all the months leading up to the event. I experienced the full benefit of their prayers. When I first began planning the event, I had a certain direction in mind. I knew we would need a powerful message to anchor the event on. I also knew I wanted the keynote to be something actionable and relevant to every woman in attendance, whether she was a teenager, an adult, a stay-at-home mom, an entrepreneur, or an employee. I wanted it to be life-changing.

Above everything else I want to mentor women to be the woman God has designed, formed, fashioned them to be. How has God uniquely wired us to fulfill our purpose on this earth? I felt it would be good to give each woman specific tools for discovering her unique purpose. The StrengthsFinder[3] assessment, a tool that helps you uncover your strengths or talents, would be a good starting point for this. I would make sure every woman would take the assessment prior to the event. I already knew our opening keynote talk would anchor this event. I had planned on doing this myself, but the women needed to hear from someone who could speak to all the different strengths that would be represented.

Stephanie Clergé, whom I knew from my years as a college intern, had reconnected over the last few years. While planning the women's event, I remembered she was a Strengths coach. I pulled up her website, read everything on it, and knew she should be our

---

[3] Gallups Strengthfinder, http://www.strengthsfinder.com/

keynote speaker. Stephanie could effectively cater the Strengths message to multiple women. I reached out to her, and she agreed.

She did an incredible job at our event. It was obvious she was in her calling as a speaker and coach. We opened the day with her keynote and on-the-spot coaching[4] for two participants. This was as life-changing for me as it was for the participants. It was clear God had orchestrated for Stephanie to be our speaker. The Strengths message truly resonated with me. It helped me clearly see how our strengths are a huge indication of why we are here on this earth.

Our strengths can be used in various professions and areas of our lives to point us to our purpose. Another word for strengths is talents. What is a talent?

Gallup's definition of a talent is "a naturally recurring pattern of thought, feeling or behavior that can be productively applied." Stephanie Clergé, our keynote speaker and President of StrengthsPRO, explains it this way: "We have such a narrow definition of talent, usually those things that people have historically become famous for doing. In reality we all have talent. Talent is just the stuff that we're made of and the stuff that we naturally do. I like to think of our talents as our personality muscles because our talents are what make us feel strong and perform in the most impactful way."

---

[4] Watch Stephanie in action at StrongerThanYouThink.co.

To turn our raw talents into strengths, Stephanie encourages us to

> *start* with the foundation of a talent. Remember those thoughts, feelings, behaviors? *Next*, you build upon that talent by adding skills, or learning the steps to complete an activity; and knowledge, or the facts or experience to do it better and better. *Add* your own interests and passions to the equation, and you have a strength. Talent is necessary but not sufficient to have consistent nearly perfect performance."

"We often do the exact opposite of this. We find that we are not that good at something and we put all of our time and attention into getting better. And maybe we do, but if it is not an area of strength for us, we only get marginally better. Rather, if we focus on areas that naturally come easily to us, areas that energize us and areas where we do well, we will be able to significantly contribute to the world. For example, I had someone on my team named Debbie who was pretty quiet and reserved, yet she was everyone's "go to" person on our team and others for her operational coordination skills. Her managers had noticed her excellent work performance and were constantly pushing her in a direction of leadership. They sent her to communication classes to help her to be more assertive and she would dutifully complete them, but she did not apply these new skills to her daily work. When

I became her manager, I too noticed her exceptional abilities in her job role. But instead of asking her to become what didn't excite her— becoming a formal leader who asserted her power and influence—we invested in additional operational training, something she was already good at. She became even better in her daily job role and was a natural but informal leader whose scope expanded with every task she completed. I nicknamed her the *Quiet Storm* because that's what she was. Powerful and influential based on an investment in her natural talents.[5]

Your strengths, your passions and your experiences help you identify your reason for being. You are the way you are for a specific reason. Knowing and discovering your strengths is not another measure of success. The quest for fulfillment through achievement can become an idol if we are not conscious of our motives and pursuits. Our motive for knowing our purpose is to be (more) effective in our God-ordained assignment.

What is your purpose? Why are you here? None of us can answer this question without God's help.

Answering this question doesn't magically eliminate pain and suffering in your life. Knowing our purpose doesn't exempt us from the hard stuff of life. We can spend years building a certain reputation in our church for being godly people. It's good to have an

---

[5] Stephanie Clergé, http://www.StrengthsPRO.com

honorable reputation, a respectable name. It's not good to allow that reputation to convince you that you won't experience trials. Your reputation through the eyes other people is not your true identity.

Jesus made himself of no reputation. We are told in Philippians 2 that even though Jesus was equal with God, He did not see His equality as something for Him to hang his hat on or use to his advantage. Instead, the greatest among us took on the form of a servant. He humbled Himself. He didn't let what other people believed about Him become the focus of His life. Instead, He thought less of what people thought of Him than what God said about Him. He found His identity in His purpose, His mission, His reason for existing. His purpose was His anchor when the storms of life came. When "his hour was at hand," His purpose saw Him through to the finish line.

God reminds us throughout scripture that He knew us long before we ever reached planet Earth. He has a plan for our being here. We were born at this specific time in history for a specific reason. We will be the most productive, will be the most fulfilled, and have the most impact when we know *why* we are here and make that the focus of our time on earth.

Water Station.

1. Do you recognize complacency in your own life? How has it held you back?
2. Make a list of ideas you've wanted to pursue in the last three years but haven't because of fear. Which one of them has the greatest potential to change your life and the lives of those around you?
3. Are you willing to risk your own comfort to take steps towards this idea in the next 12 months? Make a list of three people in your life you believe would support you to completion in your decision. Tell them about your idea.

How did it feel to tell them? Get to work!

CHAPTER 2

Lesson: Everything Would Be Different If You Changed

At the time of this writing, I've been married for 17 years. Around my second year of marriage I started keeping a journal. 1998 was the year I began to realize I needed to make some changes in the way I approached life. I needed to get intentional-purposeful.

We had moved 1,300 miles away from our family and friends to a new city. I gained 25 pounds that first year of marriage. I was going through the transition of being a wife. I was a mess and couldn't take it anymore. During that time, I listened to a message by a Christian marriage counselor titled, "If Nothing Changed Around You, Everything Would Be Different If You Changed." Only looking back do I realize this was a turning point. Parts of my thinking, my attitude, and my habits were going to have to change.

So, I went about the process of making small but immediate changes. As I'm sure you know and have experienced, change isn't as easy as it appears on the surface.

Following the path of least resistance is what's easiest. We get the least resistance in the familiar. The familiar is our default, even when it's not getting us the results we desperately want. Psychologists like Dr. Henry Cloud & Dr. John Townsend will tell you, "we change our behavior when the pain of staying the same becomes greater than the pain of changing."[6]

The changes I wanted to make back in 1998 required me to leave the familiar behind and keep moving in the direction of pain. It was painful to give up my bad thought habits. I was used to thinking wrong thoughts about my life. I would meditate on my negative emotions. Any time I had a disagreement with someone, I would still be thinking about it and beating myself up over it days (sometimes weeks) later. I had to think differently about why I was on this earth. As I read back through my very first journal, I see multiple times where it was on my heart to write a book. Here I am 17 years later, finally writing that book, and I have to wonder why it took me so long to do what I knew I should have done so many years ago.

It has taken me years to see and experience some of the things I wrote in my journal. I have to wonder: how much of those years was about God's timing and His developing and maturing me, and how much was about my own fear and resistance to change?

I have been tempted to give up on change when I wrongly assumed the path of progress would be a straight line. What about you? When you set goals at the beginning of the year, do you leave any room for mistakes or setbacks? You may have set a smaller goal of losing one pound a week to help reach a larger goal of twenty

---

[6] Dr. Henry Cloud & Dr John Townsend, *Boundaries with Kids: When to Say Yes, How to Say No* (Zondervan, 2009).

pounds. When you don't hit the smaller goal every week, do you give up on the larger goal? Picture someone you admire who has reached a goal you would like to reach. If you talk to that person, I'll bet you would find that they had multiple setbacks along the way. For those people who didn't have setbacks for that particular goal, I'll bet they did for other goals. Life requires flexibility.

I recently had a conversation with a single woman in her 30s. This woman married in her early 20s and felt she had handled her relationship "God's way," meaning she had married and had children with her husband. Unfortunately, that relationship ended in divorce. Here she was years later remaining celibate, in order to honor her commitment to again "do it God's way." She was starting to feel hurt when she would see other couples. She wondered why it was taking God so long to come through for her. In her words, she was tired. She was tired of waiting for the desire of her heart: a healthy, loving relationship with a man. I have had countless conversations with women in similar situations—women who have everything to offer, but no special man in their lives to offer it to.

I have experienced this weariness in my own life. You just grow tired of doing the right thing when you don't seem to be experiencing the benefits of your good choices. That weariness you and I feel is because we are in a fight. First Timothy 6:12 tells us we are in a fight! We are "fight[ing] the good fight of faith" (NIV). You feel tired when you are in a fight. The good news is that it's a *good* fight. Yep, you read that right! It's good. It's worth it. There's a reward.

Interruptions and detours can make you so tired that you're tempted to believe you have to give up. How many of us actually live like we believe strength and power are synonymous with living a Christian life? I believe scripture confirms that submitting to the Holy Spirit's leadership makes us strong in every way. Paul, the apostle, wrote a letter to Timothy, a younger pastor. He begins his letter by reminding Timothy that the Spirit of God doesn't make you timid or cowardly. The opposite is true. Power, love, and self-discipline are products of faith.

If you are feeling weary, weak, and tired, we are promised several things in Isaiah 40:29-31. God never grows weak or weary. God gives power to the weak and strength to the powerless. Those who trust in (wait on) God will renew their strength. That's good news! Whatever strength you've lost, and if you've grown weary because of disappointments, God can strengthen you! You are stronger than you think, because the power of Almighty God is available to you. Your strength is renewed when you trust in Him.

THREATS To Change

Procrastination

For years I had these recurring dreams that I would try to leave one place to go to another place, but something would always prevent me. I would get lost or I wouldn't have everything I needed to get where I was going or I couldn't find the people who were supposed to go with me. My dreams were a movie of my failure to complete things I started in my life. I would take off into each new venture or commitment with excitement and enthusiasm. Then when the excitement waned, or the process took longer or was harder than I imagined, I would abandon that and start something else. I didn't have any real commitment behind my actions. I wanted to try some things to test them out, but I never really planned on going all-in. I would abandon the project before I could fail, or if I did stick to it to the point of failure, I would see that as a sign that I needed to stop doing it and try something else. ⟶ *This describes me*

I once lost a job because of my failure to finish. I worked as a curriculum designer for a small company. After about a year, I found out I was pregnant. I made an arrangement with my employer to work from home and complete the curriculum project in phases, with a few months to complete each phase. My husband would ask almost daily if I was working. His questioning would make me upset, because I knew I wasn't getting the work done, but I kept telling myself I'd get it done. I continued to make other things a priority. About one or two weeks from when the first phase was due, I pulled several all-nighters. I knew it wasn't my best work, but I had left myself no options. I packaged my work and emailed it to my supervisor. She was so gracious with her feedback but gently informed me they would not be continuing on with me on this project. They still paid for the work I had done.

It was the wake-up call I needed. As a mom entrepreneur, I've had to be project manager and subject-matter expert on client projects requiring months of work. As an employee my team depends on me daily to follow through on my commitments. Without that experience, I probably would have disappointed future clients and employers.

Procrastination has been a continual hurdle for me. When I feel like I don't know enough, I procrastinate. I have an insatiable appetite for knowledge and understanding. In other words, I love to read! I've come to realize I sometimes fool myself into believing that reading and studying is the same as doing. It's not. There's a point when we must put down our books, laptops, and tablets and start executing on what we say we believe. It feels safer to read and safer to share our thoughts behind our computer screens. We've shared our *thoughts* out loud, online or in real life. That's action, isn't it? Once you've read about it and thought about it, **do something**. Our perspective is limited when we only read about a subject. When we act, we gain wisdom that we can apply to future experiences. Consider this. If you wanted a career as a writer, whose advice would you value more? Would you value the advice of a woman who has built a career as a full-time writer or a woman who's read books about building a career as a full time writer? I'm sure the woman reading the books can share relevant and timely insight, but it hasn't been proven in her own life. It's secondhand information.

When I was pregnant with our first child, I read every book I could get my hands on about parenting. I had never been a parent before, and I had no idea what to expect. I had never taken care of other children, other than my own brothers and sisters. I had, briefly, babysat for a friend a few times, but that was the extent of my nurturing children. Reading parenting books gave me insight about what it would be like to parent my own children. However, everything I read had to be proved through actual parenting. Once my own children came along, here's what I realized. Some methods in the books worked for our children, and others didn't. Learning is a good starting place for most things, but learning is solidified through experiences. The same is true for marriage. You can and should read books on marriage, but reading isn't enough. When we **act** on what we've read, lasting change occurs.

I also procrastinate when I don't know where to start or when I'm afraid of being disappointed, because the effort feels like too much of a risk. What if I put in all this time and effort into writing this book and it doesn't yield the results I expect? A few years back, while reading one of my favorite blogs, I found the word I had been trying to come up with that describes why I'm constantly checking emails, reading books or blogs, and checking social media: escapism. Escapism happens when I'm attempting to escape the work required to reach goals and realize dreams. How do I overcome procrastination? I overcome procrastination by putting in the time and effort to complete whatever task I am working on. I wish I had a sexier answer, but it's the truth.

Thankfully, I no longer have those dreams about not finishing what I started. By God's grace I've finished many things. Each time I have finished something, I gain confidence to finish the next thing.

Comparison

We are tempted to give up on change when we wrongly compare our life to someone else's life. WARNING: Comparison is a trap! It will keep you stuck in the same spot year after year after year, because it's rooted in the fear that we won't live up to expectations. It's crucial that our plans are from God and not based on what our friends and family are doing. You want your goals to be directly related to God's plan for you, not his plan for your closest friends. This attitude brings the added benefit of removing the anxiety to please people.

In the eyes of comparison you are never good enough, smart enough, spiritual enough, rich enough, or pretty enough. Comparison is one of the dream stealers. We will discuss comparison in further detail in Chapter 7: Run Your Own Race.

Complacency

Have you ever started out feeling content with the way your life was going and then, before you knew it, you were complacent? I mention complacency briefly near the beginning of this book. It's also important to highlight it here, and it will be mentioned several times throughout the book. Why? Complacency is a little tricky, because it starts off with a positive sense of being happy with the state of your life. It takes a turn when the contentment you experience keeps you from wanting to improve. Why is this problematic?

In life we are either moving forward or drifting backward; there is no neutral position. We have to be active participants in our own lives. Ultimately, your life impacts other lives. But how do you impact others, when *you're* stuck? If you are complacent, you are asleep. You may not be hurting anyone, but you are not helping anyone. You are consumed with your own life and your own needs. Complacent people have the mentality that they don't have to do it, because someone else will do it (whatever "it" is). Whatever has lulled you to sleep, I dare you to start dreaming again. I've never met an ambitious, complacent person.

Shame

2007 was a season of discouragement and questioning of God's providence. We watched the due diligence, time, and money we had invested in real estate slowly but steadily dwindle away. During this time I would continually question God and ask why He would allow this to happen. Why didn't He stop us from going through with these deals? Why couldn't He at least change the outcomes for our friends, even if He wouldn't change them for us? ***When*** was He going to change our situation and bring us out of this mess?

Every day, I expected that today would be the day we would wake up from this mess and it would all be over. I just knew that by the end of each month our situation would be different. It wasn't. Nothing around me seemed to change. In fact, it seemed to get worse. I was looking for God in our situation, and I couldn't seem to find Him.

The situation didn't change, but I did.

I could talk about the money we lost or the hard conversations we had with friends, but it was the shame and embarrassment that overwhelmed me. The shame of stepping out and falling on our faces and the embarrassment of no longer being trusted by friends was difficult to bear. You see, I am more of a rule follower than a risk taker. I had checked all the boxes. I had done all the things I thought we should do to be a success. Surely, if I had prayed, nothing bad would happen, would it?

What about you? Have you ever made a decision that seemed right at the time? Have you ever stepped out in faith and the outcome you got was different than the one you prayed for? Have you ever seen someone make a decision similar to the one you made, but with a better outcome?

I think we can all relate to the feelings of discouragement when life doesn't go as planned. How do we respond in those crossroad moments? Do we retreat? Give in? Stop pushing forward? God forbid.

Hebrews 12:1-3 (MSG) has become one of the most comforting verses of scripture for me. I believe it holds the answers to how we should respond in disappointing times:

> Do you see what this means—all these **pioneers** who blazed the way, all these veterans cheering us on? It means we'd better get on with it. Strip down, start running—and never quit! No extra spiritual fat, no parasitic sins. Keep your eyes on Jesus, who both began and finished this race we're in. Study how he did it. Because **he never lost sight of where he was headed**—that exhilarating finish in and with God—**he could put up with anything along the way: Cross, shame, whatever.** And now he's there, in the place of honor, right alongside God. **When you find yourselves flagging in your faith, go over that story again, item by item, that long litany of hostility he plowed through. That will shoot adrenaline into your souls!** (emphasis added)

When we learn and read Christ's story, it gives us the endurance we need to not give up. Romans 5:4 also assures us *problems and trials produce endurance and endurance produces character.* The lessons we are learning in this race of faith are producing character in us.

What stood between Jesus and the cross? Shame, yet, he paid it no mind. Shame really is one of the oldest tricks the enemy uses to trip us up. It takes our focus off God and puts it on us. It gets us off course. Don't believe shame. Anything that slows us down is a weight. Shame is a weight and a distraction to living a life free of regret. It is a weight to live under the fear of what others think about us. We need to throw off that fear so we are free to run towards God's promises full force.

The next time you are in a difficult situation, remind yourself of all He endured for your sake. Don't allow shame or any other weight to get between you and God. The relentless power that wouldn't allow Him to give in to the temptation to give up is the same power at work in you! You are stronger than you think! Don't give up! You're destined to win in the race of faith!

How Do We Change, When Change Is Hard?

We've discussed the threats to change. How do we change, when change is hard?

Embrace the path God has you on. How do you define success? Some aspects of success are probably beyond your control. For example, if part of your definition of success is building a business that becomes a household name, you won't have control over whether or not a celebrity mentions your business on national television. For the things that are beyond your control, you won't be able to make success happen any faster than it's going to happen. But you *can* be prepared when it comes. Ask yourself, "If my dream of _____ (fill in the blank) happened today, would I be prepared for all that comes along with it?" Who am I becoming? How is my life going to improve because of the change God is taking me through?

Be focused. Our focus should be on the things that will mean the most when our life is coming to an end. Strong relationships, a grateful spirit, and being a source of support and encouragement to other people move our focus outward to others and upward to God. Being focused in your priorities gives you momentum to reach your goals.

Be accountable. I can't tell you how much accountability has helped me in my life. I can say with confidence I am a runner. I can say this not because I'm the fastest runner or I've won awards. I can say it because I'm consistent. And I'm so consistent partially because of the amazing women who hold me accountable to running.

Be uncomfortable. Don't run from pain or discomfort. Embrace it! There is no "easy button" in life. I'm convinced one of the reasons we give up so quickly is because we get discouraged when things aren't as easy as we thought they would be. *Our confidence is weakened when we believe it should be easy and it's not.* When you feel the resistance that comes with change, do what needs to be done—even when you don't feel like it, even when you're scared, and even when you've tried it before. Do you ever hear these thoughts when you're working on your budget, lacing up your gym shoes, or calling a prospect on the phone?

I've tried this before and it didn't work (happen).

I'm not good at this.

I don't have enough money, time, experience, ___ (fill in the blank).

Yes, we all have. Combat these thoughts by speaking scriptures. Meditating on scripture has the power to transform your thinking, which will change your actions.

What area of your life have you desperately desired to experience success? Is it weight loss, raising your children, joy in your marriage, a loving relationship with your in-laws? Be honest. Have you failed in this area so many times that you're afraid to believe it's possible anymore? You've read all the books you could find on the subject. You've talked to your friends about it. You've attended seminars and conferences. You've listened to sermons on it. You've prayed and cried. Yet—NO victory.

You've Been Here Long Enough

In Deuteronomy 1:1-8 the Israelites started out on a trip that should have taken them only 11 days.

It took them 40 years!

Are you kidding me? I know what you're thinking: This can't be true. Forty years for an 11-day trip!

Consider your own life. Don't you have a similar experience?

You may be thinking, "Not me. I would never take 40 years to do something that only took 11 days."

Oh, really? Wasn't it only supposed to take you two months to lose that last 10 pounds of baby weight, but your "baby" is starting kindergarten and losing the last 10 pounds is still on your list of goals and resolutions? Or maybe you're the person who thought it should only take you a month to get rid of that bad habit, but here you are seven years later still battling with it.

If you're thinking, It's been too long. It's too painful for me to risk failing again, I've got some words of encouragement for you that come from verses 6 and 8 in Deutoronomy 1:

You've stayed at this mountain long enough. . . . Go in and take possession of the land. — But I still ask the question, "What am I to take possession of?" "What is my plan?"

Do you realize there is enough power in one word from God to enable you, to strengthen you to do whatever He's commanded you to do? What is the thing you've been told to do by God, but you keep finding excuses why it can't be done?

I say to you, *You've stayed at this mountain long enough. . . . Go in and take possession of the land.*

The idea for this book has developed over the years, but I

really scheduled time to sit down and start writing it in 2011 (then proceeded to procrastinate on finishing it for two and a half years). I've learned so much just in the process of writing the book. One thing I know for sure is when God is telling me to do something, no matter how impossible it can feel at times, He wants obedience, not excuses. He knows my schedule and my responsibilities. Writing this book has been very uncomfortable for me. Writing a book requires me to walk by faith and not by sight. Think about it. I'm spending hours of my life writing a book that has no guarantee of a reward to me (other than the reward of knowing I finished what I started).

What if you moving off the mountain in your life is more about your faith and less about your reward? The message of Hebrews 11:1-2 is, *Faith is the confidence that what we hope for will actually happen; it gives us assurance about things we cannot see. Through their faith, the people in days of old earned a good reputation.* The book of Hebrews 11 gives us many examples of the pioneers of faith. Pioneers pave the way for those who will come after them.

What are you supposed to pioneer in your life? Maybe you're supposed to be the first one in your family to go to college, finish a degree, start a business, or move out of your city. Maybe you have an idea for an invention in an industry that's been hard for others to break into. Maybe you're supposed to be the first woman to take a leadership role within your company. Maybe all of the women in your family have always worked outside the home, and now it's on your heart to be a stay-at-home mom. To pioneer is to do something you've never seen done before. To be a pioneer requires faith. Peter was a faith pioneer. He'd never seen anyone walk on water, yet he believed it was possible if God said it was possible. Esther was a faith pioneer. She believed God would be with her when she approached the king.

Will you be a pioneer of faith for those who will come after you? They need more examples of what it's like in this modern time to persevere and stretch their faith.

Godly Ambition

Watching athletes can teach us so much about this race of faith we're all in. Without even realizing it, maybe that's why we are drawn to sports. We admire the level of sacrifice, commitment, and ambition it takes to be one of the elite athletes.

Do you know the difference between contentment and complacency? A tension exists between gratitude for the good in your life and dissatisfaction with living below your intended greatness. In that tension lies the possibility for complacency.

I like the way Dr. Dave Martin puts it in his book, The 12 Traits of the Greats:

> There will always be a certain tension between what you

want and the current realities on the ground that stand between you and your destiny. This gap between what your heart desires and what your hands are currently holding will present you with two options: You can either hold to the vision until you eventually achieve it, or you can lower your expectations in order to force your dreams to match up with your current realities[7].

I believe one of the ways to address this tension is with ambition. Ambition is a strong desire to achieve success.

Did you just cringe at the word ambition? Our view of ambition has become tainted over the years. Ambition is usually cast in a negative light. We're told stories of the career-driven woman whose children take a backseat to her business success, the husband who abandons the wife who supported him for years, the back-stabbing co-worker who values a promotion above relationships. Ambition is portrayed as unhealthy and selfish. I've got news for you. If you have a strong desire to achieve success, you're ambitious. First Corinthians 9:24-27 (MSG) states,

> You've all been to the stadium and seen the athletes race. Everyone runs; one wins. **Run to win.** All **good athletes train hard.** They do it for a gold medal that tarnishes and fades. You're after one that's gold eternally. I don't know about you, but I'm **running**

---

[7] Dr. Dave Martin, *12 Traits of the Greats* (Harrison House, 2013)

hard for the finish line. I'm giving it everything I've got. **No sloppy living for me!** I'm staying alert and in top condition. **I'm not going to get caught napping, telling everyone else all about it and then missing out myself.** (emphasis added)

This verse of scripture is about an ambitious runner—a runner who wants to win. We should be asking ourselves daily, "Am I running to win?" Athletes don't just show up for their event. They've put in time and energy. They've made a commitment. Every race in life—natural and spiritual—requires faith. It takes faith to train for an event and give up things you want to do simply for the *possibility* of winning.

Sloppy living requires no discipline. It allows us to sink back into complacency and give less than our best. Paul says, Not me. I'm not going to look up and realize I've fallen behind in my own race because I wasn't living at my best. (I won't fall behind because I tell everyone about it and then miss out on living this intentional life.)

In the King James version, verse 25 of 1 Corinthians 9 states, "And every man that striveth for the mastery is temperate in all things". Runners understand striving. You can't strive unintentionally. It requires effort. It's a way of life for the athlete.

Striving takes effort. It's work. How much of our time do we spend striving for the things of this world? We spend years striving for things that will not benefit us eternally. I believe we are wired to be ambitious, but that ambition gets misdirected at some point. Instead of us striving to be like God and to live victoriously for Him, we get off track and start living for our own lusts and ambitions. In Luke 13:24 God essentially says, "If you want to strive for something, strive to enter My kingdom." When our ambitions are directed upward, God in turn directs our focus to what will please Him. We in turn live more purpose-driven lives.

Confidence

[margin note: definitely]

If you are going to make lasting changes in your life, you have to stir up the desire in your heart to want to win. <u>Have you ever wanted something so badly that you were afraid to want it, so you acted as if you didn't, even though you knew you really did?</u> If you really want to see a person's true personality come out, play a board game with her. The next time you are at a game night with friends, watch how people interact when the game starts. Some are loud and vocal about the game. We'll call them group 1, the competitive players. We all know they want to win and don't care that this is just a game among friends. Then there's group 2, those who are all into the game but don't appear to be as competitive as the first group. People in group 3 are willing to play but seem to not care one way or the other about the outcome. Lastly, group 4 finds one reason or another not to play at all. They tell themselves, I just like to watch.

When the game starts, it's easy to see the second group really is competitive. I believe those in the third and fourth groups are competitive as well, but they aren't willing to risk failure. Failure is hard and painful. As much as I think we want to be a society that admires and appreciates people who fail and get back up again, we don't. Our human nature is to judge people for failure. We love to say "I told you so" or "I knew that wouldn't work." Courage is easy to talk about but hard to live.

We see the same thing in our day-to-day lives on our jobs and in our businesses. We also see it in our churches. There are those we consider ambitious and competitive. We look at them as being too confident, wanting too much. They talk too much. They have too many opinions. Why don't they go with the flow? Why do they seem to want it so much? What are they doing, dreaming so much? Why do they think that will happen for them? Why aren't they satisfied with what satisfies everyone else? Why do they try so hard for more?

There are those we consider humble, because they don't seem to want too much.

✱My question is, are they truly humble or have they just given up on the belief that they could have more or do more?

It's important for us to think about confidence at this point. We don't truly know what it means to be confident. Confidence is directed. It is placed in or directed to someone or something.

In Isaiah 30:15 God tells the children of Israel that in quietness and confidence is their strength. They think they will find help from Egypt, but God warns them that only in resting in Him and returning to Him, getting quiet and allowing Him to rebuild their confidence, will they be strengthened. I find it interesting that God didn't just encourage them to rest in Him. He also encouraged them to be confident. <u>Confidence is not sin if it is properly directed</u>. God want us to have confidence.

We need the Holy Spirit's help to balance confidence and humility. When we make decisions, He can prompt us with questions to help us determine if our decisions are rooted in faith or fear. Humility comes from desiring God's will above our own. Our confidence comes from knowing we are asking according to God's will (1 John 5:13-14). In both confidence and humility there is an underlying belief in God's will above our own. Maybe more of us would risk being seen as confident if we truly understood what it means. Ephesians 3:12 reminds us our faith in God empowers us to come boldly and confidently to Him. Confidence is not bad. It is an expected result of our faith in God.

Water Station.

1. Look at your life. What mountain in your life have you been on long enough? Which goals, promises, or commitments have you lost confidence in your ability to achieve?
   - Writing
   - Teaching at a "good" school.
   - Becoming healthy enough
   - to bear a healthy 2nd child.
   - Becoming a lit. coach.

2. Which of the four threats—procrastination, comparison, complacency, or shame—has been hardest for you to push through? Why?
   - Print modeling
   - commercial acting

3. What is the difference between complacency and contentment?

4. Do you believe it's possible to be godly, confident, and ambitious? Name someone you know personally who exemplifies all three. Talk to this person about how he or she has been able to succeed at being all three.

↳ Who do you know, personally, that fits this bill?
- Reneé
- Rangel
-
-

THE RACE OF FAITH

CHAPTER 3

Lesson: The Runner's Secret...Endurance

The discipline and sport of running is what God has used to get my attention regarding the life of faith I live with Him. The concept for this book was planted in my heart while on a family vacation in 2010. I was on the treadmill in the fitness center, trying to push myself to keep running beyond what was comfortable. Internally, I was giving myself a pep talk. In my mind I was encouraging my body to keep going. It was hard. I was sweating and I just wanted to stop, but I knew I had the rest of the day to do whatever I wanted. I was determined to run a faster 3 miles than I was used to running. In the middle of my pep talk scripture started coming to me. "Don't faint in your mind. Don't give up." I kept repeating this over and over in my mind until I finished my 3 miles in under 30 minutes, which was my goal. When I got back to our room and looked up the context of "Don't faint in your mind," it excited me! Let me share with you what I learned.

Choose Your Training Plan

In Hebrews 12 the author uses running a race as a metaphor for life and describes the beginnings of our training plan for the race of faith. You don't decide to run on the day of a race. You prepare for the race in advance through training. Training requires discipline over a long period. You pick a training plan that will help you reach the finish line. I don't think it coincidence that God describes our lifetime with Him as a race. When I realized God was describing life as a race, I set out to learn more about what He meant by this. As a runner, I know the value of training, but training is a huge commitment of your time and your mental and physical energy. The reason most people won't train for a race is because they know they aren't disciplined enough to stay with it over time. You need a training plan that can accommodate your schedule and fitness level.

At some point most runners, regardless of their fitness level, make the decision to enter a race. They want a measuring stick for their progress or to prove to themselves they are a "runner." Most runners know they'll never win any awards for running, yet they still train. Why do we do it? Each runner is running to achieve her personal record. A personal record (PR) is your best time for a certain distance. For example, let's say you signed up for your first 5K (3.1 miles) and finished it in 30 minutes. The next time, your goal might be to beat your PR of 30 minutes. If you ran a 5K after that and finish in 29 minutes, 29 minutes is your PR. If you ran several 5Ks and your fastest time was 28 minutes, 28 minutes is your PR.

A beginner's training plan looks different from an experienced runner's plan. Beginners usually just set their goal as finishing. Experienced runners usually have a PR they would like to set. They may even have a goal of being one of the first three finishers for their age, gender, or overall. The plan you choose to be a finisher of a race is very different from the plan you use to finish at the top. Either instance requires a time commitment to train to cross the finish line injury-free. Both overtraining and undertraining can cause injury. The bottom line: training for a race requires a certain level of discipline and commitment that many people are not willing to make.

As a new believer you may start out your walk with God with a simple desire to make it to the finish line of the race of faith. Somewhere along the path on your journey with God, you start to desire more. You start praying about His purpose for your life; you start serving in your local church; you stop gossiping with your girlfriends; you start reading your Bible daily; you start looking for other women to disciple; you start sharing your faith with your co-workers and your family; you change the channel when that reality show you used to enjoy comes on. You've essentially changed your training plan. Your desire has shifted from just wanting to finish, to wanting to win!

The Race of Faith

Therefore, since we are surrounded by such a huge crowd of witnesses to the life of faith, let us strip off every weight that slows us down, especially the sin that so easily trips us up. And **let us run with endurance** the race God has set before us. We do this by keeping our eyes on Jesus, the champion who initiates and perfects our faith. Because of the joy awaiting him, he **endured** the cross, disregarding its shame. Now he is seated in the place of honor beside God's throne. Think of all the hostility he **endured** from sinful people;[c] then you won't become weary and give up. After all, you have not yet given your lives in your struggle against sin. . .

No discipline is enjoyable while it is happening—it's painful! But afterward there will be a peaceful harvest of right living for those who are trained in this way.

(Hebrews 12:1-4,11 (NLT), emphasis added)

Every race has a crowd of people supporting the runners. To hear other people cheering for you, supporting you when you are growing tired during the race, can be just the burst of energy you need at times to keep going. Hebrews encourages us that we are not alone. We are surrounded by other believers, living and not living, who've had to run this same race.

Our crowd has a seat to witness our life of faith. This life of faith can't be seen with our physical eyes. It happens in the realm of the spirit. The scriptures reveal many things about faith:

You Are Stronger Than You Think

- Without it, it's **im-poss-ible** to please God.
- We only need a small amount to see mountains moved in our lives.
  - It gets tested.
  - It's dead without corresponding action.
  - It makes us whole.
  - Anything not of it is sin.
  - It's the confidence that what we hope for will happen. It gives assurance of the things we cannot see.
  - It can be examined to see if it's genuine.
  - It can waver and it can flourish. *I sometimes feel it does this on a daily basis.*
  - It can be great and it can be little.
  - We need it to be saved.

Some of the skimpiest outfits you will ever see can be found at your local 5K race. In case you hadn't noticed, runners dress comfortably, but light. We don't dress this way to show off our great bodies. The goal is to minimize anything that could potentially slow us down. What slows us down from running the race of faith? Sin. Sin trips us up. How does sin trip us up? Sin destroys our confidence that we can approach God. Sin opens the door for pride which makes us think we no longer need God. Sin keeps us looking at our mistakes with regret instead of keeping our eyes forward. We'll discuss this more in a moment.

In Hebrews 12 we are given specific instructions to run with

endurance the race that has been set before us. Endurance is a concept runners know well. It's vital to the life of any athlete. You must endure to reach the finish line, finish the game, or reach the goal. This word is used three times in some form in Hebrews 12:1-3. Endurance is obviously an important concept in the life of faith. Let's dig a little deeper into its meaning.

> *endure*: suffer without yielding; suffer patiently;
>
> to undergo (hardship, strain, privation, etc) without yielding; bear
>
> *origin of endure*:
>
> late 14c., from O.Fr. endurer, from L. indurare "make hard," in L.L. "harden (the heart) against," from in- "in" + durare "to harden.[8]

Jesus endured the cross, and He endured hostility. We are required to endure on a smaller level. To endure you have to suffer. Anything that requires you to endure requires you to suffer, to undergo hardship or strain. This makes so much sense. The very word itself is letting you know it's not going to be pleasant. We falsely believe that running shouldn't be hard, but it is. It's as hard for the person at the front of a race as it is for the person at the back.

What's even more interesting is the origin of the word: to make hard, harden (the heart) against, to harden. Having to endure hardens

---

[8] Definition of Endure, http://dictionary.reference.com/browse/endure

us to suffering. Training requires us to endure long workouts, long runs. The result is that we get harder. We're able to bear up under the strain of training until we can run longer and faster.

We run this hard race by keeping our eyes on our champion, Jesus Christ. Imagine this: *You're in an arena, at a race, and the crowd is cheering. You're pushing yourself harder than you ever have before. The sweat is pouring down your back, your chest, and your face. Your body is telling you to stop, but your spirit is saying keep going. Just when you feel like you can't go anymore, you look up on the screen and see your champion, Jesus Christ, seated at the right hand of the Father. He's reassuring you that He's run this race before and He knows how hard it is to be where you are, but He's telling you if you will just keep running and keep your eyes on the prize that is set before you, you will finish. You realize that through His example and encouragement, He's distracted you from all the things that have tried to stop you from making it to the end. You realize you are finishing the race and everyone who has supported you is there.*

It isn't just your imagination; it's a reality for ever believer who will persevere.

One more key truth about this verse. The Amplified Bible translation of Hebrews 12:2 states, "*Looking away [from all that will distract] to Jesus, Who is the Leader and the Source of our faith [giving the first incentive for our belief] and is also its Finisher *[bringing it to maturity and perfection]."* Jesus leads, He finishes, and He is the Source of our faith. He's the reason why we believe, and He's given us the ability to finish this race.

Run Toward the Goal and Don't Look Back!

I have not achieved it [perfection], but I focus on this one thing: Forgetting the past and looking forward to what lies ahead, **I press on to reach the end of the race and receive the heavenly prize for which God, through Christ Jesus, is calling us. (Philippians 3:13-14 (NLT), emphasis added)**

In this passage Paul profoundly declares he focuses on one thing—the future. This is the man who wrote two-thirds of the New Testament. Paul gives the key principle for staying focused as we run the race of faith: forget what's behind us and keep our eyes forward.

Running a race can be hard. Sometimes it's hard because you didn't train as much as you should have or because you didn't go to bed as early as you should have the night before. Other times the race is hard because it's a tough course.

I've never seen a runner win a race while looking back. In fact one of the big "no nos" of running is looking back to see what's happening behind you. Looking back slows you down. You shift your focus from the finish line to what's happening around you. Can you imagine if Jesus had taken this approach to the cross? If he focused on the fact that Judas betrayed him for money? What if he had focused on the fact that one of his closest disciples, Peter, denied knowing Him at a time when He needed Him most? If Jesus had been focused on the past instead of the future that God was taking Him into, He would have opened Himself up to faint in His mind. He could have allowed the pain of betrayal, rejection, and abandonment to keep Him from His destiny. This is as true for us as it was for Christ. <u>We are running a race and can't afford to hold on to a past that will try to drag us down with regret</u>. We have a heavenly prize for which God is calling us upward to receive.

For he [Esau] could find no opportunity to repair by repentance [what he had done, no chance to recall the choice he had made.] (Hebrews 12:17 (AMP))

The truth is, we all have a track record, with ourselves and with other people, of the mistakes we've made. <u>When we blow it with people, the quickest path to forgiveness is humility</u>. We must be willing to humble ourselves and ask for forgiveness of the person we've wronged. Hebrews 12 is the cautionary tale of Esau's life and a reminder that even when we are forgiven by those we love, we should be careful of making choices that cannot be reversed. In those times we have to remember Paul's example and stop looking back, in order to move forward.

Fight for It!

Multiple fights happen at every race you attend. You'll miss it if you don't look carefully. It's a fight between the mind and the body. It's most visible when a runner has surpassed the halfway point of a race. As a runner you are constantly gauging how your body feels. *How's my breathing? How do my legs feel? Am I tense or relaxed? Do I need to stop for water or the bathroom? If I don't stop, will I regret it later?* Sometimes during a race, the mind and body seem to work together, and other times they seem to be at odds. This is when the fight happens. You are fighting to keep going to reach your goal. In the race of faith our fight is the *good* fight of faith. Good meaning a fight worth having, because it allows us to hold on tightly to eternal life.

The prize for fighting the *good* fight of faith and finishing our race is revealed in 2 Timothy 4:7-8: "I have fought the good fight, I have finished the race, and I have remained faithful. And now the prize awaits me—the crown of righteousness . . ."

Fight to the finish. The reward is worth it!

Water Station.

1. Have you shifted from wanting to finish in the race of faith to running to win? If so, what life event triggered this change?
2. List the names of some of your biggest supporters in the race of faith. Next to their names, write how they have supported you. Call, email, or text each one individually and thank him or her. — Grandma
— Charnita
— Sherry
— The Ladies of Epiphany's Circle

CHAPTER 4

Lesson: Be Ready to Run

Running (or any sport) requires mental toughness. Running the race of faith requires a disciplined, self-controlled mind. Our thought life can be the difference between finishing a race with a personal best or giving up before we make it to the finish line. This chapter provides strategies for mentally preparing yourself to run your race.

Are You Mentally Ready?

January 2007 I ran my first half marathon. I had been running for a few years and had several 5Ks under my belt. Since I started running I had always had a dream (I had no plan to put behind it) to tackle a big goal like running a half marathon. I knew if I could run a half marathon and finish, it would inspire me in other areas of my life. Around June of 2006 I saw a flyer in my gym stating that a group would be training for the Rock 'n' Roll marathon in January 2007. All running levels were welcomed. The cost included registration and a carb-loading dinner the Friday prior to the race. I was sold. A running group was exactly what I was looking for. Group work of any kind is motivating to me, and I knew I would benefit from the accountability. I went home, told my husband about it, gulped down my fear, and signed up. At our orientation they explained we would be training from September to January. We would run together two days during the week in the evenings, and our long runs would be on Saturday mornings. We would train on our own the rest of the days. I walked away excited and committed to seeing the plan to the end. Our training started two weeks after that first meeting.

I showed up ready to go. There was a group of about 20 of us. As we took off running, I quickly learned I was one of the three slowest people in the group. I was fine with that. We were only running a mile and a half that day.

The excitement of training for a half marathon caused me to start out too fast. About halfway into it I felt like I wasn't going to make it to the end. It was as if I had never run at all. I barely squeezed out that mile and a half. I was so happy when it was over. Every time I ran for the first few weeks, it was like that. Doubts started creeping in: How are you going to run 13.1 miles if you can barely run 1.5? Each week our mileage would increase and each week I felt sure I had bitten off more than I could chew.

Then, one day it happened. About six weeks into training, I realized I would be panting and fighting everything in me not to stop for the first two miles—but after the first two miles I would feel my body relax and settle into the run. It wasn't easy and it wasn't comfortable, but I knew my body would keep going. Week after week I could feel my endurance building. I was getting stronger and faster. I was no longer at the back of the pack; I was in the middle. People started dropping out of training for various reasons: injuries,

[Margin note: I currently feel like I lack discipline in a lot of areas of my life.]

lack of time to train consistently, and others.

Training for a marathon, half or full, requires a real commitment of time and energy. If you under train, you can get injured. If you over train, you can get injured. If you're going to train for a half marathon you have to get acquainted with a word that many of us don't want to hear, let alone live, *discipline*. On many of my training runs I would say to myself, "Why are you doing this?" The reality is that there were days when I just didn't want to train anymore, but I needed to honor my commitment to myself. I didn't want the satisfaction of giving in to my flesh when things were hard. Not finishing what I started was a real problem for me. Quitting projects when my excitement waned was my norm. Therefore, this wasn't about me training for and running a half marathon. Training for that race taught me what it means to endure, to persevere!

You know what else I realized during that time? We have an amazing capacity to experience contentment and peace in the midst of pain and suffering. It's how we are able to endure tough times and not lose all hope. It's truly miraculous!

That year we went back to our home state of Louisiana for Christmas. I managed to keep training, but not as much as I had been. I had been training about 14 weeks at that point. I actually needed that little break from intense training. I didn't need the extra food I ate, but hey, you only live once, right? Anyway, when we got home I had about two weeks of training left. Before I knew it, it was

You Are Stronger Than You Think

race day. I was ready. I felt really good about the training time I had put in. I was faster than I had predicted I would be when I registered. Therefore, at the starting line, I was able to move up ahead of some of the other runners (at big races you are lined up according to your anticipated run times). Exciting!

The weather decided to throw us a curve ball that year. The morning of race day set a record for being one of the coldest mornings ever in Phoenix. It was 32 degrees in Phoenix! Can you imagine how the Kenyan runners felt? For us thin blooded Phoenicians it was beyond cold. They taught us the warnings signs for hypothermia, and we were off. A great sense of pride washed over me. I had set a goal 18 weeks before and was ready to fulfill it. To tell you it was hard would be an understatement. To run for that long at that temperature was one of the most challenging things I've ever done in my life. For 13.1 miles my hands were ice-cold. I only allowed myself to stop at one water station halfway through for a sports drink. I felt that if I stopped too much I would stop running altogether. Your training and adrenaline carry you through the first eight miles of a half marathon, but the last five take pure determination. I was glad I had trained. I knew my training would see me through to the end, but it was hard. At mile 10 I didn't think I could keep going. I wanted to cry or scream, but that would have taken too much energy.

Crowds play a huge role in a race. The cheers, the signs, the applause are so encouraging when you are giving it everything you've got to make it across the finish line. Finally, after 2 hours and 23 minutes, I had completed my first half marathon with a faster time than I planned. This was a moment of pure joy for me. I felt invincible! I had run my race and finished my course.

Who Has the Last Word?

Whether you're a runner or not, I'm sure it doesn't surprise you that running requires mental and physical stamina. Both overtraining and undertraining can lead to injuries that sideline you from your race. How you prepare determines whether you finish injury-free and whether you finish at all. It's a given that training helps you physically condition yourself to run. But did you know there is mental conditioning involved as well?

You can mentally talk yourself out of running before your body needs to stop. Beyond physical conditioning, your long runs condition you to keep going, mentally. Your mind will tell you to stop. Why? We live by resolutions we've made in our hearts and minds based on our past experiences. An internal conflict happens inside of us, when we want to make changes in our lives that bump up against these resolutions. In *Captivating: Unveiling the Mystery of a Woman's Soul*, Stasi Eldredge refers to them as vows:

> The wounds we received as young girls did not come alone. They brought messages with them, messages that struck at the core of our hearts. . . .The vows we make as children are . . . essentially a deep-seated agreement with the messages

of our wounds. They act as an agreement with the verdict on us. "Fine. If that's how it is, then that's how it is. I'll live my life in the following way . . ."

What resolutions or vows, beneficial or detrimental, do you live by?

When you run, a conversation takes place between your mind and spirit. It sounds similar to this:

Mind: *Why are you doing this in the first place?*

Spirit: "I discipline my body like an athlete, training it to do what it should. Otherwise, I fear that after preaching to others I myself might be disqualified" (1 Corinthians 9:27 (NLT))

Mind: *Why are you up at 5:30 a.m. getting dressed to go running when you could be in the bed sleeping?*

Spirit: If I walk by the Spirit, I will not fulfill the lusts or dictates of my flesh. (Galatians 5:16 & Romans 8:1)

My goal is to always let the spirit have the last word. Did you notice the body is not in the conversation? Where the mind and spirit go, the body will usually follow. With the proper training and conditioning we are physically capable of far more than we know; just ask Roger Bannister, the first runner to run a mile in less than four minutes. Experts believed his achievement to be impossible.

Roger is quoted as saying, "It is the brain, not the heart or lungs, that is the critical organ. It's the brain."[9]

In training, the two hardest moments for me are getting out of bed and getting out the door and into those first two miles. In both instances there's an internal battle:

Why don't you sleep for just 30 more minutes?

Could you do this at a different time of the day?

Give yourself another day to recover.

I'm bored with this.

Why does this feel so hard?

I'm tired; just walk. Running is too hard.

Choose another exercise easier than running.

Why do I have to do this to stay in shape?

You've been doing this long enough.

Ask someone else to lead the running group today so you can sleep in.

All of these thoughts go through my mind, and they will continue to

---

[9] Timothy David Noakes, "Fatigue is a Brain-Derived Emotion that Regulates the Exercise Behavior to Ensure the Protection of Whole Body Homeostasis, Frontiers in Physiology," http://www.ncbi.nlm.nih.gov/pmc/articles/PMC3323922/. (April 11, 2012)

happen.

Some days they are valid and I give in to them, but most days I don't.

In chapter 3 we talked about the training plan. I want to shed more light on this truth in Hebrews 12: "Think of all the hostility he **endured** from sinful people; then you won't become weary and give up" (Hebrews 12:3 (NLT)).

Many times we faint—grow weary and give up—in our mind before our body gives out on us. In many instances, we don't finish what we start or live out our purpose and callings, because we have first given up in our minds.

> Even youths grow tired and weary,
>
> and young men stumble and fall;
>
> but those who hope in the LORD
>
> will renew their strength.
>
> They will soar on wings like eagles;
>
> **they will run and not grow weary,**
>
> **they will walk and not be faint. (Isaiah 40:30-31 (NIV), emphasis added)**

Renew Your Mind

A water station is an opportunity for a hot, weary runner to get refreshed. Most runners are strategic about how they plan their stops and know better than to run an entire race without stopping for some type of liquid refreshment. Throughout this chapter I have shared numerous scriptures. Spending time in the scriptures provides the refreshing our souls need when we grow weary in the race of faith. They keep us strong. How often we stop for these times of refreshing along our course can determine whether we make it across the finish line.

Through reading and studying the scriptures we renew our minds. Renewing the mind is key for every Christian, but it doesn't happen without a plan.

Here's how you make scripture reading a priority in the race of faith:

Don't let anything interfere with it. Stop thinking you don't need a plan; if you don't make time for it, it's probably not going to happen. Have a specific time of day that is free from distractions where you meet God with your Bible.

Run with other believers. Get together with other people to discuss the scriptures on a regular basis. The camaraderie and accountability of meeting with other believers helps you stay focused and committed. This doesn't have to be an in person meeting. It could happen with the use of some online tool like a private Facebook group or even over the phone.

This sounds like a good idea.

Persist when your mind tells you it's not making a difference. You can feel like you hydrated before a run because you drank a glass of water, but that's not enough. Puffy fingers from edema are a sign that a runner's dehydrated. We don't always see the effects of our choices until they've already set in. Reading the scriptures is not optional in the life of the believer.

The Word makes a difference, because it:

- o Reveals our true motives (Hebrews 4:12)
- o Is full of life (John 6:63)
- o Gives instructions (2 Timothy 3:16)

What Are You Training For?

The race of faith requires all of you. We are to be controlled by the Spirit, but if we don't engage our mind we will faint and be finished before we ever really get started. The body has a part as well. It's not all mental and spiritual. You can have the mind and spirit engaged, but you have to act. Faith and action are no good apart. One inspires the other. One supports the other. James said it this way: "show me your faith without the works, and I will show you my faith by my works" (James 2:18 (NASB)).

Are you preparing to launch a business?

Are you raising children?

Are you preparing for a long and healthy marriage?

Are you preparing to lose weight?

Are you preparing for a career change?

Are you preparing for an empty nest?

What actions have you taken towards this?

> Do you need to take a class?

> Is there someone you need to meet with?

> Are you out of debt or working on getting out of debt in preparation for it?

Do you have a Proverbs 31:25 perspective? Do you look to the future with peace and with a smile because you know you and your family are prepared? If not, what would it take right now to get prepared? It may take a series of steps. Let this book be the inspiration and the reminder you need to keep running the race with patient endurance.

I'm convinced many of us are missing the corresponding action that goes with our faith. We've been crying out to God, "Lord, how long?" and He's responding, "Yes, daughter, how long?"

What Is Your Why?

Giving birth is such a monumental event in a woman's life. It takes you through a range of emotions. I clearly remember what it was like giving birth to our first child, our daughter. My emotions ranged from fear to excitement to irritation to gratitude. All of these emotions fluctuated throughout my body for the 12 hours I spent in labor with her. Weeks before, my husband and I had taken labor classes that coached us on what to expect and how to handle labor. One of the techniques was to have a focal point, an object I should focus my attention on when the contractions started to overwhelm me. I decided it was too tempting for me to give in to fear during labor, so I decided I needed a focal point that had some meaning.

When we were happy and excited about the new life we were going to bring into the world, we went out and bought things for her room. One of the first things we bought was a little patchwork rabbit. It was lime green, light blue, and yellow. I brought that little bunny to the hospital with me. It was my focal point. It was my why. One of the descriptions of labor pains is *pain with a purpose*. This made so much sense to me and gave me the motivation I needed to get through labor and delivery. I had rehearsed the reasons for the pain I was experiencing. I knew that every time I experienced a contraction I was getting centimeters closer to holding her in my arms. It was pain with a purpose. Even though that did not make the pain or the process any easier, it changed my perspective which helped me stay focused. The focal point was a symbol, a marker for me of *why* I was going through the pain. There was a little baby girl on the other side of that pain, and that made it all worthwhile!

What is your *why*?

Your why is your passion. It's your fuel, your stamina. Starting with why you want to do something is always a good first step, because it keeps you focused on the end result. The focus we gain from having a clear purpose behind our activities keeps us grounded. It is the internal motivation we need to keep pressing forward.

There is a why, a reason, for everything you've experienced in your life. The why makes it worth anything we have to go through to arrive at a more fulfilled life.

Many days will be routine. You'll have a plan to follow. Other days you'll have to fight for. Sometimes even when you fight for them, those days won't go as planned. Don't abandon your commitment because life looks different than expected. Whatever you do most of the time is who you are.

Lasting change happens when we shift from an instant-gratification mindset to a lifestyle mindset. One of the greatest benefits of running is the way it continuously challenges what I've set as priority in my life. I'm convinced one of the primary reasons we continue to fall short of our goals is because we look at them as tasks to accomplish instead of commitments to real change. With all we know about nutrition and exercise, the reason we continue to be enticed by rapid weight-loss diets is because we need the high of reaching a goal quickly. But let me ask you a question. How painful is it when you lose that 10 pounds in 3 weeks and then gain it all back as quickly as you lost it? We all do it. We're all praying for God to deliver us quickly out of or give us the answer to our situation. We want the high of a quick rescue. We resist having to persevere at a new habit until it becomes a lifestyle.

How would our lives be different if our prayer life wasn't about us praying frantically to deliver us from crisis to crisis?

What if prayer was our lifestyle where we lived in constant communication with the Lord? What if daily fellowship with Him was how we lived?

Do you think we would have more peace when hard situations raise their heads in our lives? I believe we would.

How do you make anything a lifestyle? You practice. You live it daily, no matter your emotions that day. It has to be a priority in your day. You make time for whatever it is. You stop making excuses. As you already know, we all have the same 24 hours of the day. Why are some people more productive, more effective than others? I would be willing to bet it has to do with how they spend their daily lives.

I think of time like money. There is a limited amount that we get to spend each day. Time is probably more valuable than money because we can get more money but we can never get more time.

Once you've spent it, it's gone. I want you to be honest with yourself and evaluate how you're spending your time. <u>Is there room for improvement?</u> I'll bet there is. I'm dedicating an entire section to this because this is the number one area that has held me back in my attempts at reaching goals. I've wasted so much of the time I've been given. I am the type of person who hates waste. I really don't like to waste food, resources, time, or anything else of value, but I have. I've allowed countless hours of procrastination to keep me from choosing the better things in life.

YES!

As I'm writing this I'm reminded of familiar story in the Bible. I'm sure you've heard it explained in many different ways, but I'm realizing there is a hidden truth I've overlooked before now.

> Now it came to pass, as they went, that he entered into a certain village: and a certain woman named Martha received him into her house. And she had a sister called Mary, which also sat at Jesus' feet, and heard his word. But Martha was cumbered about much serving, and came to him, and said, Lord, dost thou not care that my sister hath left me to serve alone? bid her therefore that she help me. And Jesus answered and said unto her, Martha, Martha, thou art careful and troubled about many things: But one thing is needful: and Mary hath chosen that good part, which shall not be taken away from her. (Luke 10:38-42 (KJV))

But Martha was cumbered about much serving. The New Living Translation says, *Martha was distracted by the big dinner she was preparing*. Martha was doing a good thing, right? Yes, but she was doing it at the wrong time. Because she was serving when she should have been worshipping, it's interpreted as a distraction. She was worried and concerned over the details when she should have chosen the better thing to do in that moment. The better use of her time in that moment was to worship her Lord. This opportunity may never have presented itself again. Can you relate to this in your own life? I know I can. The plans that are truly life-changing are those we've surrendered to the Lord's timing.

Believers talk a great deal about God's timing. We've used it as an excuse to do nothing. What does it mean to surrender to God's timing?

Wait on the Lord

Patience—endurance—is not something I enjoy. One of the reasons I've started over so many times is because I haven't had the patience to see the outcome I desired. Think about it. Who enjoys waiting? Waiting is not fun. You can become anxious in your waiting. Do you remember waiting as a kid for someone to come pick you up? Every car that drove by sounded like the one. The good thing is, you were in expectation for the person you were waiting on. You were in faith. You knew they were coming; you just didn't know when. Isn't that the hard part about waiting on God? You know He's going to come through for you; you just don't know when.

I've often wondered about this idea of God's timing. Part of me felt like it's a myth or something we say when we don't know why things aren't happening according to our timing.

As I searched the scriptures, I believe there's a strong case for "God's timing" being a boundary that we all live and work within.

What is the significance of God's timing in the race of faith? David speaks frequently in the Psalms about waiting on God. Waiting on God helps to sustain his faith. In Psalm 27:13-14 David is confident that He will experience God's goodness and His deliverance from His enemies while he is still living. In Psalm 62 he again confirms his expectation that God will come through for him. As a warrior, David lived in constant threat of danger. Every second mattered. Most of us will never know what it is like to live this way. Yet, David is vocal about his confidence in waiting patiently for the Lord to answer him.

In Habakkuk 2:3 there is an encouragement that "This vision is for a future time. It describes the end, and it will be fulfilled. If it seems slow in coming, wait patiently, for it will surely take place. It will not be delayed."

Jesus says to His disciples in John 7:6, "Now is not the right time for me to go, but you can go anytime."

This truth that Jesus spoke is confirmed in Galatians 4:4-5: "when the right time came, God sent his Son, born of a woman, subject to the law. 5 God sent him to buy freedom for us who were slaves to the law, so that he could adopt us as his very own children."

What are the benefits of waiting on the Lord? Isaiah 40:31 tells us we can expect renewed strength.

If you are feeling weary, could it be that you aren't *waiting* on the Lord? I get it. I know from experience. We are human. We sometimes grow weary in our waiting. God assures us of at least two things:

We can come to him. Our burdens are not too much for him. This is Jesus' assurance from Matthew 11:28-30.

He will come through for us. In Lamentations 3:25-26 we are assured the Lord is good to those who wait patiently for him.

What is our part? How do we wait expectantly in a season of life that we wish would end? We all have the ability and capacity to endure. We are talking about patient endurance. You don't grow tired in doing what's right. You endure with a good attitude. You have faith God is going to come through for you. In the following chapters we will discuss strategies for how to endure in your most important relationships, in your daily life, and when waiting to see your dreams become reality.

Water Station.

1. In this season of life, what are you training for, that is, wanting to start? What action have you put behind this?
2. What is your approach to prayer? Is it a lifestyle or a last resort?
3. What does waiting on the Lord mean to you?

② It's not a last resort, but I feel like it's haphazard.

③ I'm still unsure of what to do while I wait. I sometimes think that if I am focused on the here and now while I wait, that I am not keeping my faithful vision in sight. Then, if I focus too much on my faithful vision, I'm not showing pleasure in the blessings God has already given me.

CHAPTER 5

Lesson: Persevere In Your Most Valued Relationships

These next two chapters on endurance (endurance for relationships and to follow God's leading) were the hardest chapters to write. It's difficult to put into words, how to keep going when you feel like giving up. A determination develops, internally, that's difficult to explain. I don't think there is a formula you can follow. There is no "one size fits all" answer for endurance. It takes practice to endure. It takes experiencing pain over and over again, feeling your faith muscle break down and having it repair until you gain the strength you need to keep going. I consider these principles, more than rules or even standards. You might have some of your own to add to the list. Above all, I pray for you to experience a renewed sense of hope while reading through these chapters and that something, even if it's just one thing, will make the difference for you.

Choose the Right Training Partners

In November 2011 I ran and finished my second half marathon with a slightly lower finish time than the first. There's a big gap between my first my second for multiple reasons. In 2008 I got pregnant with and gave birth to our third child. Unlike I did for my first half marathon, in 2007, I tried to train on my own. My training was so inconsistent I never registered for the race. In 2010 I was determined

I was going to train for and complete my second half marathon. Around this time a friend expressed her own interest in training for a half. We set up a time to meet weekly to run together. Our relationship grew stronger and closer during this time. Some of my best conversations have happened while running. Our time was the highlight of my day, but at some point I realized at the rate we were training we wouldn't be ready for a 5K, let alone a half marathon. Our "running" time didn't really involve that much running. We had opposite attitudes and approaches to running. I followed a schedule and still ran on the days when we didn't "run" together. She only ran when we were together. The result: every time we ran together, which was only once or twice a week, it was like her first time. We were catching up and connecting, which was great, but there was no way I would be ready for any race.

Races aren't run on intention. You can't finish or win a race based on what you intend to do. It's what you actually do that matters. I had to find a group who enjoyed running. I had to connect with people who were in the mindset to train for a race they wanted to finish.

The following year, 2011, I became the leader of a running group. Can you believe it? Me, the woman who could barely run a mile and a half, was now encouraging other women to reach their fitness goals. Our first group run in August was to begin a 10-week training plan to run a half marathon that November. We did it! I did it. I wanted to quit at mile 8, but I didn't and crossed the finish line with one of the ladies I trained with. My time was 2 hours and 22 minutes, about 13 minutes more than my goal, but I was still happy with the time. I had trained and not only finished but about four other women I had helped train finished too.

Use Peer Pressure to Your Advantage

Peer pressure isn't always negative. It can be used to our advantage. Witnessing the success of other people can be a source of our greatest motivation. It's one of the reasons people love success stories. It's why support groups work. It's the reason why most people run faster during a race than they do in training. Athletes understand a little healthy competition can be just the boost you need to help you achieve a personal best.

Running appears on the surface to be a solo sport. When you're in a race, the only way to finish is for **you** to run. No one else can finish the course for you. However, one of the best things about being a runner is the support of other runners, including your running partners. The high fives and the words of encouragement are acknowledgements, one runner to another. You understand what it takes for them to be out on the pavement giving it their all.

Success stories help us believe we can succeed. It's inspiring to see other people jump over hurdles we seem to keep tripping over. It becomes unhealthy when we allow fear in the form of jealousy or envy to creep in. Jealousy is fear that God won't come through for us as He has for someone else. Fear is sin, because fear opposes and tries to contradict our faith.

It's valuable to put yourself in positions where you depend on other people and other people depend on you. Accountability is really what I'm talking about. Being not just a member but a leader of a running group has been my accountability. The women in the group inspired me to run longer and faster. I've signed up for races that challenged me and brought to the surface things I didn't know were in me. I show up to run every week not just because of the sense of accomplishment I feel when I'm done, but because I know people are depending on me. I've been a more consistent runner and a more dependable person as a result of running with a group.

Endurance to Stay Married

Being married requires endurance. Entire books have been written about marriage and the requirements for a healthy marriage, and there's no way I could do it justice in just a few pages. I will share how my husband and I have been able to persevere in the last 17 years of marriage. I thought it appropriate that he would help me write this section of the book.

[Daniel]

Marriage, like most other critical relationships, is like a long-distance race. As with any long-distance race, many factors must be considered before the race begins. We don't just jump on the starting line the day of the race expecting to make it to the end, just because we showed up and paid our fee to be there. I used to run three miles a day back in college and I can assure you, I needed plenty of preparation to run the whole distance. Kendra now runs half marathons, and even more prep is needed to do that. Whenever we get ready for a race, we must drink plenty of water, eat the proper food for the right nutrients, and gradually build up the endurance of our muscles. So, how does this all apply to marriage? Glad you asked. Marriage is, literally, the end of life as you know it as a single person and the beginning of a whole new life. Everything changes. If you are prepared for a race, you have experienced bruises, muscle soreness, blisters, aches, and pains. Why? Your body, to a certain degree, breaks down to build up and get ready. In marriage, it's important to take the steps necessary to transform ourselves from a person focused on self to a person ready to make someone else the focus.

Entering into a marriage covenant is one of the best and most painful ways to learn that life is not all about you! This realization comes pretty quickly after the wedding day. When you begin to wake up next to, spend all day with, and go to bed next to the same person every day of your life, you really begin to understand how selfish you are. Selfishness is one of the first (what I call) marriage character flaws that stuns couples in the beginning. I remember the early years of our marriage being a time of reckoning. "I reckon she will figure out how to fold towels one day. I reckon she will figure out how to fold socks one day. I reckon she will learn that dust isn't going to just get up off the furniture one day."

We learn about marriage through our parents, grandparents, uncles, and aunts—and all of us have very diverse experiences. In my house growing up, my mother did things a certain way, and I thought that was the way it should be done in my marriage. I didn't think maybe I could be open to doing some things differently. My attitude in the beginning came from the fact that the way I grew up was part of my identity and changing that meant giving up part of who I was, or so I felt. What I was missing was that as a married man, I was now coming into my own and starting a new journey where I now could forge my own way. I began to understand that my focus was misplaced. What we focus on grows. As long as I remained focused on the how and not the why, I would remain frustrated and would have continually frustrated Kendra. I had to take a step back and realize that towels and socks were revealing my selfish tendencies, which were keeping me off center of where I really needed to be. I had a paradigm shift from focusing on how or what my experience was in the past in my parents' home to creating a new experience in my new home with my wife. Here's a tip for young married men. Ready? Drop the phrase "My mother." It is no longer about what happened in your momma's house. It will only exacerbate the problem, and it only serves to turn your selfishness on full blast. If you really want to live with the way your momma does it, you should have stayed with your momma. The Bible commands us to leave our father and mother and cleave to our wife. Go ahead and come up with new ways to do things. Marriage is a new season, and it is time to do a new thing!

If you've ever tried to run long-distance, one word comes to mind when it comes to finishing. That word for me is focus. You have to focus in order to get from start to finish, because there will be all kinds of internal and external distractions. A race may be very cold if you decide to run in a January race in the Midwest or very hot if you choose a summer race. Maybe you experience cramps along the way, or get light-headed from running at higher altitudes. Regardless of the conditions, when race day comes you must fixate on running your race, not on the distractions. No matter how much you have trained, the race will always have a few unanticipated distractions along the way. You may have to talk your way through a distraction or make an adjustment during the race. You never want a cramp or the weather to become the focus. When it does, it takes your mind, will, and emotions away from the goal of running the race.

Focus in marriage is also important. Without focus, there's a tendency to isolate yourself from your spouse. Because we are naturally inclined to be selfish, we must focus on strengthening the bond between each other from day one so that we avoid the drift of isolation and enable closeness and togetherness and oneness. As I mentioned earlier, what we focus on grows. All an idea needs to become reality is our focus. Focus means to concentrate or to centralize your efforts toward an outcome. It is proven that humans don't multitask very well, so attempting to focus on the negative and positive at the same time doesn't work. We either want a great marriage that will endure, or we don't, or somewhere in between. We must decide to create a great enduring marriage and then focus ourselves on that decision.

We have to look at our interaction with our spouse very carefully. We want the love, tenderness, intimacy, and caring for one another to be our primary focus. We want those relationship-building things to be big in our marriage, not the things that cause us to drift apart.

[Kendra]

For nearly two decades my husband and I have served in a leadership capacity in our church home. I currently serve in a leadership capacity in the women's ministry. We both serve, together, in the marriage ministry as well. We also lead an online group for married couples. Through our years of talking with and serving married couples, we see certain commonalities among couples who endure and other commonalities in those who grow weary and burn out in their marriages.

Enduring couples are . . .

tender and honorable with each other. They choose their words wisely. They are respectful in word, tone, and attitude towards their spouse, even when they disagree. They understand that life and death are in the power of the tongue and they can use their words to either build their spouse up or tear them down. Our communication style has to adjust to fit the needs and *love language*[10] of our spouse. We need to be planting seeds that will produce the type of harvest we want to reap.

realistic towards their spouse in their expectations. You are going to have disagreements in marriage. You are going to have hurt feelings. You are going to be disappointed. Don't be surprised and don't sweep your disappointment under the rug hoping it will go away. For your marriage to endure life's challenges, you must be willing to talk through the tough stuff of life. It won't just go away. Talk about everything. Even when it's hard.

focused on the good. What is right about your spouse? Why did you marry him or her? What do you love most about your spouse? This is where our focus should be.

willing to accept and give forgiveness when needed. Some days you will need forgiveness. Some days your spouse will need forgiveness. It is impossible for two flawed people to

---

[10] *The 5 Love Languages* by Gary Chapman. If you haven't read it, get it!

live together without a need for forgiveness at some point. Don't keep score of your spouse's mistakes. When you do, you both lose.

aware of God's greater purpose for their marriage. What are your strengths? How do they benefit your spouse? What are your spouse's strengths? How do they benefit you? What does God want to accomplish through you as a couple that wouldn't happen, separately? If you don't know the answer to this question, start praying about it. *God has a plan for your marriage!*

[VERY MUCH SO!] **picky and discerning about the people they bring around their marriage.** The right friendships are important to the health of any marriage. Who are your closest friends? Are they a help or hindrance to your oneness relationship with your spouse?

students of their marriage. They have a library of marriage resources and are always looking to continually improve their marriage.

Married couples can burn out or grow weary in their marriages when...

one or both of the spouses is a know-it-all who is not open to seeing life through the other's point of view.

yelling at each other is the norm.

a harsh, critical, sarcastic atmosphere is the norm.

their primary focus is on vanity and vain pursuits.

they hold grudges and keep an account of each other's mistakes.

there is no desire to get into your spouse's world, to learn their likes, dislikes, hopes, dreams, fears, and passions.

These are not exhaustive lists, because all marriages are different. We all come to marriage under different circumstances. I hope this list would inspire you to become a student of your own marriage and you would look for opportunities to make your marriage one of the ones that endures.

Endurance to Raise Our Children

We are currently raising a 6-, a 12-, and a 13-year-old. If any area of your life requires endurance, it's parenting! The development and care of another human being is exhausting work. I thank God daily for His strength in this area of my life.

My go-to scripture as a parent is Galatians 6:9. It is a promise from God's Word that I keep before me daily. When I'm really tired and feel like checking out mentally, I remind myself that we are only blessed to have them live with us for less than a quarter of our lives.

As the saying goes, *the days are long, but the years are short*. Our top priorities as parents have been to raise men and a woman who fear the Lord, care about others, and uncover and nurture the gifts and talents God has placed on the inside of them. I ask God to help us not grow weary in this privileged assignment. We believe our children are arrows in our hands and God has given us the assignment to launch them out into the world. <u>As we launch them out into the world and they leave our hands, our job was to have created a home environment that set a solid foundation for spiritual and personal development and academic success.</u>

We have such an important role as parents. The things all children learn in the early years truly shape who they become as adults. Think about your own life. It's really difficult to change who you are at your core, once you leave your parent's home. The things we learn, the habits we formed, and the way we approach the world greatly influence our view of life. Our home life growing up taught us how to interact with other people and maneuver around in this world.

There is a temptation to disengage as a parent, especially when we don't have perfectly behaved children. **How do we endure as we parent our children?**

I feel strengthened in my assignment as a parent in a number of ways:

We learn to parent by becoming a student of our

children. When we see behavior we don't like, we help them work on their character. Character is the root of how we develop in life. It determines the choices we make. Our character is the real us when no one is watching.

When our oldest daughter was a pre-teen we began to notice a change in her behaviors and the way she responded to situations. We have always been the type of parents who look for parenting mentors, whether it's through people we know personally or from parenting books. As we observed this shift in her, we knew we needed to shift our parenting. We attended a class at a local church titled, *Train Up A Parent: How to instill biblical character into the hearts of your children.* One of the primary things we learned was the role of parenting in our children's character development. According to Scot and Holly Anderson, the author of the text we used in the class, character is "the thoughts and beliefs that issue your behavior, your inner qualities that set your action. It is what we are really like when no one is around, who we are when no one is looking, what we are willing to do that no one can discover. It is the heart of man, that part which God is concerned. God doesn't look at the outside. He looks at the intent of the heart. He looks at the character of man."[11]

---

[11] Scot Anderson, *Train Up A Parent: How to instill biblical character into the hearts of your children.* (Living Word Bible Church, 2012)

In their early years, children depend on their parents' observations to know where they need to grow. Their childhood is spent building a foundation for future development. I'm willing to be so bold as to say, if we spent the majority of their childhood helping them do nothing else but develop their character, we will have done our jobs as parents.

As our children get closer to leaving our home, they should begin taking ownership of their own development. This may not be in leaps and bounds, but in small baby steps. They have a lifetime of development ahead of them.

We are honored to have the privilege of training up children. I know it can be a daunting task, but that's why God has given us grace to be the parents they need us to be and we can't grow weary in doing what's right.

How do we persevere and make the most of the time we have to raise our children?

Lean on God for wisdom and strength. I can't tell you how many hours I spend praying for every aspect of my children's future, including their decision-making abilities and their ability to clearly discern God's voice above the noise of this world. I have referenced a book over and over again, while they are growing up. *The Power of a Praying Parent,* by Stormie Omartian, has been a staple for me. I have prayed through every prayer in that book multiple times for all three of our children. Praying for my children does not mean they will not make mistakes and do things that make me wonder if God heard my prayers. I don't pray for them to be little robots who do everything perfectly and make me and their father look like "super-parents" to our friends and family. I pray for them because I wholeheartedly believe God hears and answers my prayers for their protection and guidance. I also pray because I want God to be real to them. In prayer I get God's wisdom and understanding of how my husband and I can make our faith tangible, in hopes they will continue on this path of following God. One of my prayers for them and my friends' children is that nothing this world has to offer them will compare to what they know about God for themselves. "Let the little children come to me," Jesus says in the book of Matthew. Children are a gift from God. They are our heritage. They remind us of the innocence of our faith.

Join or create a community for raising our children. There is a weariness about parenting today. Parents seemed checked out. We are all working so hard and moving so fast. I believe part of this disconnect is because we're no longer raising our children in community. We are going it alone. Many families don't live in the same communities anymore, so we are left on our own to raise our children. Both my parents and my husband's live in Louisiana. I have a sister who lives in New York and a brother in Colorado. My other two siblings and my husband's two siblings live in Texas. We have no biological family in Arizona where we live. Our church family and our friends are our community. (For a few years my husband's brother and one of my sisters lived in Arizona.) When our kids were younger, we built a strong support system of friends around us. Otherwise, I have no idea how we would have had dates or been able to do anything as husband and wife without our children along. We had to build community out of necessity, but it's one of the best things we could have ever done. <u>We would be exhausted parents with frustrated children, if all of their experiences revolved around their time spent with us. You will grow weary as a parent if you are the only source of support and entertainment for your children.</u>

A lesson I am still learning.

One of the ways we initially built community was through small groups. We were small-group leaders for over a decade. Even though we are no longer a part of a formal small group that meets weekly, we continue to build relationships and friendships in other ways. We are always looking for opportunities to connect with other couples. We invite people to our home and accept when we are invited to their homes. We carpool with my son's best friend's family. We take our kids to birthday parties and invite their friends to their parties. All of these simple things you are already doing help build community. Building community doesn't need to be burdensome. It will benefit your entire family, if you are willing to put in the time and effort it takes.

Raise your children with an eternal perspective. It's not enough for me just to pray for my children. They have to take ownership for their own spiritual maturity. I can only do so much. We need to be intentional rather than reactive as parents. What is the end result of the moments we have with them? We live in a time when so much noise distracts from our role as parents. We have technology at our fingertips all of the time, and these gadgets tempt us to escape from the realities of life and parenting. We have human beings to raise. They deserve our time and our attention. They will only be children for about 25 percent of their lives. We can't check out on them. We don't want everything they learn to come through experience. There's so much to teach them and not much time to do it in.

Let go of any unrealistic expectations that we have of our children and ourselves. Sometimes I wish I could pour my 39 years of wisdom into my children to prevent them from making the mistakes I've made. I do share the wisdom of my experience when I can, but I'm also learning to let them fail when they choose to go their own way. They have to learn what it feels like to fail and that failure doesn't have to break them. Good can come out of failure. Most of what we learn that benefits us and propels us forward was because of mistakes we made. Part of our kids learning that they are stronger than they think is learning that failure doesn't have to define them. I say let them fail under your leadership. Our homes are a safe place for them to learn how to recover from setbacks.

I have been downright embarrassed by some of the choices that I've seen my children make. Each one of our children has an area of life where he or she is tempted to make bad choices. One of our children is tempted to lie and hide things from us. The other one is very honest but deals with the temptation to have a negative attitude. It is painful at times to watch them attempt to make decisions, but quality decision-making is a muscle we all have to develop through our own choices. How will our children ever learn to make decisions, if we are afraid to let them fail? We wear ourselves and our kids out if we always step in to rescue them. We also send them the message that we don't believe they can handle it when things don't turn out the way they (or you) expected. Perfection is too great a burden for any of us to bear. When did perfection become the goal of parenting?

Water Station.

1. Which qualities of an enduring couple do you see in your marriage? What, if any, qualities would you add to the list?

2. Describe the perfect parent. Describe the perfect child. Can you live up to this standard? Can your kids? Where did this standard come from?

① As the years go by in our marriage, I find that we talk to each other more and more. We sincerely desire honest and open communication with each other because we genuinely care about each other.

② I honestly don't know perfect parents. But I have observed good and bad and I believe we are trying to do the best by our daughter that we possibly can.

CHAPTER 6

Lesson: Having It All Is Exhausting!

I still remember the day my closest friend called crying because her toddler daughter had another ear infection. She wasn't crying because of the ear infection. She knew her ear would heal and her daughter would be fine. She cried because she had to leave work ... again. She felt her co-workers were starting to think she couldn't manage the responsibilities of being a mom and a career woman. I'll bet she was probably wondering the same thing. *Been there!*

I will not put myself in a position to think I know all the reasons why women are employed, entrepreneurial, or completely devoted to raising their children as their work. I have been a full-time stay-at-home mom and a work-at-home mom entrepreneur, and I currently work outside of the home full-time. I was a stay-at-home mom the day we sat on the phone, and my friend was employed full-time outside the home. As we talked, God gave me words to encourage her. I shared with her that God's grace was available and possible to help her be both a mom and a working woman. I've been sharing this same encouragement with women for years. I made a vow, years ago, to withhold my judgment and criticism of a mother's choice to work inside or outside the home. Generally speaking, we fiercely love our children, our spouses, and our families, and every decision we make in life somehow comes back to how we are best serving them.

When I made the shift to working outside the home in July 2013 after having worked as a work-at-home mom entrepreneur for five years, I knew the transition wasn't going to be easy. I knew there would be a change in the way my household ran and the expectations my husband and I placed on our children and each other. I will tell you there have been some hiccups, bumps, and a few bruises on this journey. I've had to face my fears and my doubts about doing both and "having it all." My learning curve as a business woman, a wife, and a mother have all increased significantly. I've been asking myself and God questions about what other women and moms in similar positions are experiencing.

The relationship status of women and work in my world is complicated. Surprisingly, I believe the topic of women and work is still taboo in the Christian community. As a community, we are more understanding of women who work outside the home out of necessity. When a woman chooses to be employed outside the home or own a business because she enjoys work beyond motherhood, that's hard for people to understand. There are unspoken questions: Why would you choose that? Why isn't being a mom enough for you? If both parents are working outside the home, who's raising the kids? *[handwritten: I get some variation of this question often. I even ask myself from time to time —]* I've watched women who, the moment they get engaged, start planning when they could quit their jobs. Why does marriage shift our ambition towards work? If I'm not mistaken, all of my closest friends stopped working full-time at some point during their marriage. I'm curious. Why is this? What expectations are we placing on our marriage? Once we start having children, the likelihood that we will leave the workforce only increases. The length of time we are gone from the workforce also increases.

My own work history has been greatly influenced by marriage and motherhood. I worked part-time and finished my degree in the early years of my marriage. Once we started having children, I became a full-time stay-at-home mom. This was always my dream and desire. My choice to stay home meant greater flexibility and freedom to be available for our young family. As my children and I got older, I realized I needed and wanted the best of both worlds, the income and creative energy of working combined with the flexibility of being home with our children. My passion for business was ignited! I've had multiple home-based businesses through the years.

These days I work full-time outside the home and work from home one day a week. When I write, the professional working woman, employed or entrepreneur, is usually my source of inspiration. I know, from experiences in my own life, the demands on her time. I also identify with feelings of never quite doing enough for your work and your family and sometimes even God. The truth is, my work matters to me and I enjoy getting paid for the work that I do. I am thankful to be doing challenging, interesting, and purposeful work. I believe my work and my purpose are connected.

On any given day my state of mind, like that of many working women, can be summed up by a cartoon I sometimes share at the beginning of presentations:

I am Woman. I am Invincible. I am Tired.

I wrestled with this section on endurance for working women, because I know so many women are searching for answers to the question, "How do I do it all?" Whether you run a business from home, are employed full- or part-time from home, or work outside the home, it's going to be tough while you figure out what works for your family.

Here's what endurance looks like for me in this season of life. It requires some juggling. My priorities may change on any given day, but my values won't change. For example, I spent the last quarter of 2014 finishing this book, in the midst of finishing a six-month project at work and volunteering at my church. As I was heading into that hectic season, I talked to my husband about it. I let my family know what to expect, and we all agreed that I would shift my focus to work longer hours for the last few months of the year as I wrapped up all these projects. It was a stressful season. I did some good work, but I'm glad that season has ended. I set expectations early on and put a deadline on that time of life. <u>I could not continue at this pace indefinitely.</u> Create a pace that works for our family —

All around me, I see so many women who are tired, frustrated, and ready to give up on the idea of working professionally outside the home or running a business. Does quitting your job really give you the result you want, long term? I've been there, and it didn't for me. We talked about expectations in chapter 5, and I think this is a good place to bring them up again.

I have shifted my expectations and let go of the idea that for life to be enjoyable, it has to be easy. There can be an ease to life that feels right for my family, but the work to get there may not be easy. I'm learning to embrace the realities of this new season. There are things that I was able to do as a work-at-home mom that I'm unable to do now that I work outside the home. The summers have probably been the most difficult adjustment for me. I wrote about this on a blog, for which I'm a contributing writer:

When I was home, I had the flexibility to register our children for a variety of activities from swimming to Lego robotics classes to ceramics. Even when I had a home-based business, our summer days consisted of daily swimming lessons plus trips to the zoo and the science center and community center classes. We took lengthy road trips, spent plenty of time at the library, and met up with friends for movie nights and play dates.

There's a temptation at times for me to free-fall into guilt and condemnation over our decision for me to work outside the home full-time. One of the greatest blessings, however, to come out of this season has been the increase in the amount of time our children spend with my husband. My husband has always been an involved dad. Yet, in this season of life our roles overlap more than they did when I was a stay-at-home, work-at-home mom. He and I depend on each other so much more now than we did before.

He takes our boys to school every day. He reschedules his meetings or leaves them early, so that one of us could be there for our kids' classroom activities. He takes planned and sometimes unplanned vacation days to spend time with them during their school breaks. My husband's presence and commitment in the lives of our children is one of the things of which I am most thankful. [12]

Thank You God for Osborne :)

At a marriage retreat last summer we took the time to talk through and pray about the ups and downs of this new normal for our family and we arrived at the conclusion that my continuing to work full-time is right for us (for now). I still wonder (like every mom on the planet), if we are making the right decision for our kids. My heart is open to God's leading and I trust we will know when this season is ending. We've had some really good days and some not so great days, but as a family we are experiencing God's grace, His wisdom, peace, and joy along the way. *I'm not alone.*

As women, our frustrations often surface when we feel like our spouse isn't helping enough or we feel guilty that he's having to help "too" much. Our commute is too long. Our job isn't fulfilling enough. We're missing out on too much of our kid's lives.

---

[12] "God Is Doing Something New" by Kendra Tillman, http://deeperwaters.us/god-is-doing-something-new/. November 11, 2014

Remember in chapter 2 when we talked about godly ambition and the gap between where you are and where you believe you should be? That is the gap you are in. That tension will exist, indefinitely, unless you define what's important to you, adjust your expectations and start asking for help.

I spent too many years of my life putting pressure on myself to do everything on my own. Working outside the home has stretched me and forced me to realize I can't do it all on my own (and I'm not supposed to do it alone). As a result, I've gotten better at asking for help when I need it. Getting help for me meant learning to delegate. An approach I learned years ago from one of my favorite authors, Lysa Terkeurst, was to divide my commitments into 3 simple categories:

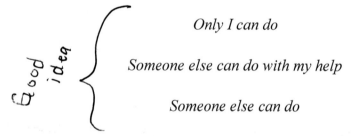

Only I can do

Someone else can do with my help

Someone else can do

Only I can love and encourage my husband and children. *Only I can* keep my body in good shape. *Only I can* show up for work everyday (unless you know something I don't). *Only I can* write this book.

An example of someone else can do with my help is typically the chores we give our kids do each week. Primarily, our youngest needs my guidance with chores. The older two are pretty self-sufficient with the exception of laundry. We noticed bleach stains on underwear, towels, pants and shirts. I wondered if one of the kids had spilled bleach in the washing machine. After a little detective work we learned our daughter was washing loads of laundry in bleach, because she didn't know the difference between bleach and detergent! Doh! Needless to say, this is one chore I check up on...frequently. *LOL!*

I delegate things I may be able to do myself, but it would save me time, effort and energy, if I allowed someone else to do it. For example, house cleaning and laundry are things we do, but they can also be things *someone else can do*. From time to time we hire a maid service or laundry service to come in and do the work for us. We have an accountant who does our taxes. Why would I spend hours of my life doing something I'm not very good at? Scheduling regular hair appointments with my stylist is also a responsibility I delegate at times. I can take care of my own hair and most times I do, but when our life speeds up this is one of the things I like to delegate.

Realizing I don't have to do it all by myself has been liberating for me. How about you? Do I have your wheels turning? Make a mental note of things you can start delegating to relieve the pressure you feel to do it all.

Here's one final thought. A vital source of strength for me in this season of life has been building my own community of friends who are in similar seasons of life. I'm a relational person, which is why this works so well for me. I thrive in group settings. Not having the weight of figuring it all out myself energizes me. What energizes you? There are people around you who feel confident and satisfied in their choices. What counsel have they already shared with you to help you get the help you need, but you haven't followed through? Your next step doesn't need to be anything big or bold. It just needs to be a step in the direction you want to go in.

Water Station.

1. Are you enjoying your life more than you are tired from it? What's one thing you can move off your 'to do' list to a family member, friend or colleague this week?

   Tired most days ↗

2. What were/are your expectations of how you would manage working while keeping the commitments to your family? Do you need to adjust your expectations?

① The biggest thing I need to move off my list is WORRY.

② I have to adjust my expectations going into this new school year. I expected to feel in full and complete control 100% of the time. I need to cope better when circumstances take control out of my hands.

CHAPTER 7

Lesson: Run Your Own Race!

"I say this all the time: I don't look at myself as standing in Oprah's shadow, I see me as standing in her light." – Gayle King

Our culture breeds comparison. We're constantly looking over at those around us and gauging our success in comparison to everyone else's. Unknowingly, we even set goals not based on our true desires or God's desire for us but on what we hear or observe from other people. It's impossible to run your own race if you're looking over your shoulder. What would happen if we stopped comparing ourselves to one another and started celebrating our uniqueness? The goal of this chapter is to describe how we overcome the hurdle of comparison, so we can run the race God has designed for us to run.

While writing this book, I had a conversation with my sister about comparison. Her frustration was with Facebook, specifically. She realized her discontentment with her life was in proportion to the amount of time she was spending on Facebook. She is a single woman over 30 with a good life, but she saw her friends getting married and having children, something she wants for her own life. She saw people dating and thriving in their dream careers, again desires she has for her own life, but they aren't happening in the time frame she desires. Am I saying people shouldn't share the joys and triumphs, the blessings in their lives for fear of how it might make other people feel? No! My concern is more directed at when you're witnessing the blessings of others rather than when you are receiving them. If we aren't careful, we can become discontented and frustrated because we aren't really looking at our lives but at someone else's. It's impossible to run your own race when you keep your eyes on what someone else is doing or what's happening for them instead of being grateful for what's happening for you.

In every race it's bound to happen. Unless you are the faster runner on the course, someone is going to pass you by. Their training has prepared them to be able to run past you. You can't let their passing you discount what God is doing in your life. Getting passed will trigger one of two reactions: discouragement or inspiration.

Is your environment causing your discontentment? Who are you surrounding yourself with? The company you keep does matter. The relationships in your life can either empower you or drain you of your ability to stay focused. There are 3 types of people you want around you in the race of faith:

Those You Run With

When you run long distances, it's inspiring to look over at people running the same pace as you.

If they can do it, I can do it. I won't let them stop and they won't let me stop.

Those who run at your same pace serve as a form of accountability. You all get to grow together. Encouragement and establishing a foundation of disciplined living is one of the benefits of running with those at your same pace.

Let's pause and talk about accountability for a moment. I think accountability is overused and misunderstood, so much so that it has started to gain a negative connotation. What's the first word that comes to mind when you hear accountability? For too many of us it means judgment. It means someone in my life is going to tell me how I'm not enough.

What does it really mean to hold people accountable?

How do the people running at our same pace hold us accountable? Accountability partners don't let us off the hook. They remind us of the commitment we've made to ourselves on days when it feels easier to give up than to keep going. They **empathize** (not judge) with the pain of discipline necessary to reach our milestones. They are there to celebrate those milestones when we do reach them. What area(s) of your life do you seem to continually keep coming up short? Do you have someone in your life who's working towards your same goal or who has already reached the goal you're reaching for? Are you accountable to anyone? The accountability that comes from people having common goals and wanting to see each other succeed could be the missing element that is holding back your progress.

You can experience improvement when you run with those at your same pace. However, to accelerate your improvement, it helps to stretch yourself and run with those faster and stronger than you.

Those Who Are Ahead of You

It never fails in every race. Someone I wouldn't have expected comes from behind and runs right past me. It might be a mom with a jogging stroller or a woman in her sixties with the stamina of a twenty-something. I've learned those ahead of me can either inspire me or intimidate me. It's my decision. When I keep the right perspective, they inspire me to improve. They are a reminder of what's possible.

It seems in every phase of my life I end up with close friends who excel in their area of expertise. My best friend has been a financial coach for ten years. I have watched her progression over the years. I still remember when she first made the decision to leave a well-paid corporate position and start her own business. She was concerned about whether she was making the right decision. Flash forward a decade to the other side of her decision. To see all that she has achieved, as a result of her passion for helping families and her obedience to God's leading, is inspiring!

I also have a friend who is an engineer by profession and the author of a cookbook that has won local awards. She is known for her spirit of excellence and her passion for healthy eating. Rhonda?

Another close friend is one of the most dynamic people you'll ever meet. She is clearly operating in her gift. Everyone she comes in contact with seems to feel empowered by her. She's charismatic, confident, and gifted at helping other people tap into their purpose. She is the epitome of a life coach. Isha?

Each one of these women has a very specific way she helps people live better, more fulfilled lives. When I observe people who are talented in ways I may not be, I have to be careful not to compare myself and allow pride and jealousy to make me wish I had their talents. *I am ashamed to say that I feel this way at times.* One of the best ways to counteract jealousy is by building confidence in your own unique calling. The course you run in the race of faith will look different from those around you.

Comparison is a form of ungratefulness. Ungratefulness always blocks the blessings in your own life. Having a healthy body and mind is a blessing. The blessings don't stop coming in your life because of ungratefulness; you just stop recognizing them. You can't thank God for the good in your life when you're focused on what's happening for someone else that's not happening for you.

For nearly two and a half years I hosted an online radio show for work-at-home mom entrepreneurs. During that time I interviewed about 30 women who were succeeding at the work-at-home mom lifestyle of both raising a family and rocking a business. (For old episodes visit thesavvywahm.com)

I would also record audio blog posts from time to time. In writing this chapter, one particular episode came to mind. The episode was titled, "Your Standing Ovation Is Coming."[13]

Here's a brief summary:

> *Have you ever wished your own gift was more . . . you know . . . celebrated?*
>
> *Maybe your gift is not the kind that causes people to outwardly stand to their feet in ovation, but that doesn't make it any less valuable. . . .*
>
> **Your standing ovation is coming . . .**
>
> *Think of your favorite singer. There are so many people operating in the background. People we don't recognize. People who, if they weren't there, would hinder our experience with the artist.*
>
> *Have you ever read a book that changed your life? Your actions, behaviors, or attitudes were different as a result of reading that book. The author is to be commended, but so are the people who edited the book. What about the publisher? The publisher is to be commended for having the*

---

[13] Kendra Tillman. "Your Standing Ovation is Coming." http://thesavvywahm.com/wahm-success-radio-recent-episodes/wahm-success-radio-show/ (Good Life Diva Communications, 2013)

ability to recognize and invest in talent that could be shared with the world.

You can probably name an actor or comedian whose work you enjoy. You've seen all their movies. You get excited when you see them being interviewed. What about the people behind the scenes who wrote the scripts?

It takes everyone completing their individual purposes for us to experience the fullness of all that even one of us is capable of.

What is your gift? Are you the one who has an ability to look at an issue and get to the heart of the matter? Are you the person who can bring order out of chaos? Are you someone who has an ability to help draw out the potential in others? Look for ways to maximize your gift.

Where has God gifted you to create ovation in the hearts of others?

I think part of our envy and comparison comes because we can't recognize our strengths and what makes us wonderfully different.

One of the tools I've found that has helped me discover what's special and different about me is the StrengthsFinder assessment, I mentioned in Chapter 1. StrengthsFinder is an assessment by Gallup that helps you measure your strengths or talents. Something as simple as discovering your strengths can help destroy the root of comparison.

You've got to trust that God knows why He has you on this path and ask the Holy Spirit to empower you to run it with endurance.

Appreciate and be grateful.

Acknowledge your progress.

Run to win!

Those Behind You

... as we let our own light shine, we unconsciously give other people permission to do the same. –Marianne Williamson

Sometimes your best motivation comes from a determination to strengthen those who are following you. If you ever decide to run a marathon, full or half, you will probably see someone running with a wooden pole with a paper that has a time written on it. The time on the pole is the time the pace setter expects to finish the race. The pace setter is expected to run at a steady pace during the race and serve as a marker for those wanting to run at that pace. Following this person gives you a marker to follow when you are unsure if you are on track for your expected finish time.

I've always told people that running is mental sport. Many times your body can go the distance, but your mind is telling you to stop. Before you ever start a race you've set a goal for how fast you think you can run that race. You then spend weeks or months training for your race. In a long distance race like a half marathon, it's helpful to have someone you can focus on, someone to follow during the race. During the race, the pace setter allows me to focus on running my race rather than wondering if I'm on pace for my goal.

I've been blessed throughout my life to have "pace setter" women I admire. Our immediate family has lived about eleven hundred miles from us our entire marriage. We were married on a Saturday and moved to Arizona on a Monday. For nearly 18 years we have been on our own as husband and wife and now as parents. I feel truly blessed to have both a mother and mother-in-law who have been wonderful mentors to me. Despite our living so far from family, God still provided ongoing mentorship and a different perspective through the relationship I have with another wise woman who has been in my life for nearly the same amount of time that I've been married. She and I have read many books together on parenting, marriage, finance, time management and goal setting. Her family was the first I ever met that homeschooled their children. Homeschooling was not the education route we chose. I still learned many parenting lessons just from observing how she and her husband raised their four daughters. We've had the privilege to watch her daughters blossom into the adult women they are today. Even during this season of her life of being a grandparent, she and her husband still take time to meet with my husband and I, just to talk parenting. I'm so grateful for her example.

In this season of my life I desire to be a "pace setter" for other women. My life experience as a wife and mother has graced me with wisdom that I know other women need. I am now in a season of mentoring other women in their roles as wives, mothers and career women. Mentoring doesn't always happen one on one. Some of my best mentoring sessions have happened through reading books that provided instruction or insight that I needed. If you are reading this book and you are not as far along on your parenting or marriage journey as I am, I hope this book will mentor and encourage you to not give up.

We all have our own race to run. We may not welcome the responsibility of having others depend on us, but it's important. Don't be timid in your approach to life. Who needs you? Your life example or your words of encouragement could be the motivation someone needs to keep running in the race of faith!

Water Station.

1. Where has God gifted you to create ovation in the hearts of others? *Teaching ... I think.*

2. In the race of faith, who is "ahead" of you that you want to learn from? Have you reached out to them? *- Rachelle - This author*

3. Look around you. In what ways are you further along the path than others? Who is looking to you as a source of encouragement? Identify one person you can reach back to this week and offer encouragement. *-RayJean (?) - My new co-worker (?)*

CHAPTER 8

Lesson: Finish Strong!

Finishing is better than starting. Patience is better than pride. – Ecclesiastes 7:8 (NLT)

It's bound to happen. You are going to get tired. There will be days when you feel like you have nothing more to give. Yet, deep down you will sense more is required of you. May these last three parting truths stir a sense of hope in you that God's grace will see you through to the finish line.

Truth 1: Surround yourself with the right support in the form of people and resources.

Have you grown weary?

Guard your heart above all else, for it determines the course of your life. (Proverbs 4:23)

How do we guard our hearts? We are told, in verses 20-22 of that same chapter, to give attention to our Father's words. Listen to His words. Don't let them depart from our sight. Keep them in our hearts. Guarding your heart is right in step with chapter 4 about mentally preparing to run.

What we believe or think about our situation can determine whether we give up, lose heart, or keep fighting. Finding a scripture (or scriptures) can anchor our souls to so we don't quit. Also, finding stories of people who inspire you could be a reminder of what's possible.

Truth 2: Stop feeling sorry for yourself.

I am well acquainted with self-pity. During the writing of this book, when I was still working from home, one day my two boys stayed home from school with cold symptoms. Our youngest was a toddler at the time. This particular day, instead of putting down his brother's game that he was obsessed with, he sat on our couch and peed on himself. I was ready to go through the roof. After I cleaned him up and finally calmed down, I gave him a cup of juice without a lid, because I couldn't find the cup with the lid. He's pretty good about drinking out of a cup, but before I knew it, he had knocked over the cup. I thought my head was going to explode (it didn't). I calmly poured him another cup while rehearsing in my brain: mistakes happen. As soon as I poured him another cup, he knocked that one over as well, and this time it spilled on the floor, too. At that point I was ready to tear my hair out and lock him in his room. (I did neither.)

While in my room getting something to clean it up, I had a nice pity party for myself. *Lord, why? I can't get anything done. Why bother with cleaning up? The house was clean and after one day of them being home it looks like a tornado went through it. I give up. I quit. What difference does this make? It would be so much easier to have them at school all day and for me to go to a regular job.*

Do you hear how irrational my reasoning became? Can you relate? You may be facing situations that are much more dire than your child having accident on himself. My hope is the humor of my situation will remind you to look for the truth in your situation. <u>Self pity brings unwelcome guests into the home of our hearts.</u> It brings resentment, selfishness, fear, and the threats to change we discussed in the beginning of the book—particularly comparison. These unwelcome guests taint our view of reality. On days when I'm tempted to devalue my progress I return to the lessons I've shared in this book and I hope you will do the same.

Truth 3: Sometimes it takes more faith to go slow and steady than sacrificing for a short period of time and finishing quickly.

> Be assured and understand that the trial and proving of your faith bring out endurance and steadfastness and patience. But let endurance and steadfastness and patience have full play and do a thorough work, so that you may be [people] perfectly and fully developed [with no defects], lacking in nothing. –James 1:3-4 (AMP)

I understand the rush that momentum can give when we get focused and intent on a goal so we can finish quickly. I'm not saying this is wrong. But I think we also have to acknowledge when we're supposed to go at a slower pace.

I started this chapter quoting Ecclesiastes 7:8: "Finishing is better than starting. Patience is better than pride." Separately, both of these sentences make perfect sense, but why are they in the same passage? What does one have to do with the other? I believe God is saying that sometimes going through the training, the preparation, the process is His will because it teaches us to endure through life's temptations, tests, and trials. Sometimes when we finish too quickly, we can step over into pride. Pride blocks the learning that comes with humility. It puts us in a position of exalting our efforts and making judgments about why other people aren't in the same position as we are. Pride stops the learning process. Part of what we gain by going through a process is allowing patience to have her perfect work, so we could be perfectly and fully developed, lacking nothing. This process keeps us from falling back into old habits and patterns. We start to form new ones that help us support the better life God is taking us to.

My prayer is that this book has been a reminder of the value of an eternal perspective. I pray it will be one of the training manuals God will bring across your path in the race of faith. Like Paul and like Christ, may we all be able to say, "I have finished my course …"

Water Station.

I began this book talking about regret. Regret produces sadness. It is a mourning of something we wish had or had not done. I don't know about you. I hope to live my life with no regrets. Wouldn't it be great to come to the end of your life knowing you had done everything you wanted to do and said everything you needed to say to those you love and care about? Guess what? None of us is promised another day on this earth. Take some time this week to examine your life. Who would you regret not being able to see or talk to another day? What would you regret leaving this earth unfinished? Go do it!

ABOUT THE AUTHOR

Kendra Tillman is a new author, an event host and director of the *Stronger Than You Think Women's Event*. The *Stronger Than You Think* Event is a premier event to equip professional Christian women with biblical wisdom and encouragement for succeeding in life and business, while informing girls 12-18 of the many career opportunities available while expanding their vision of Godly leadership. Visit http://www.StrongerThanYouThink.co for more information.

Kendra is focused on equipping women with the strategies they need to succeed in business and as the keepers of their home—from the work life dynamic, to integrating your work and your faith, to courageous entrepreneurship. Kendra and her husband, Daniel, are the parents of three children and make their home in Chandler, Arizona.